HOW *to* GIVE FINANCIAL ADVICE *to* WOMEN

Attracting & Retaining
High-Net-Worth
Female Clients

Kathleen Burns Kingsbury

New York Chicago San Francisco Lisbon London Madrid Mexico City
Milan New Delhi San Juan Seoul Singapore Sydney Toronto

The *McGraw-Hill* Companies

1 2 3 4 5 6 7 8 9 0   QFR/QFR   1 8 7 6 5 4 3 2

ISBN 978-0-07-179897-6
MHID 0-07-179897-8

e-ISBN 978-0-07-179898-3
e-MHID 0-07-179898-6

Library of Congress Cataloging-in-Publication Data

Kingsbury, Kathleen Burns.
How to give financial advice to women : attracting and retaining high-net-worth female clients / by Kathleen Burns Kingsbury.
   p. cm.
ISBN-13: 978-0-07-179897-6 (alk. paper)
ISBN-10: 0-07-179897-8 (alk. paper)
1. Investment advisors—Marketing. 2. Financial planners—Marketing.
3. Women—Finance, Personal. I. Title.
HG4621.K52 2013
332.6068'8—dc23

                                                                2012017103

This publication is designed to provide accurate and authoritative information in regard to the subject matter covered. It is sold with the understanding that neither the author nor the publisher is engaged in rendering legal, accounting, securities trading, or other professional services. If legal advice or other expert assistance is required, the services of a competent professional person should be sought.
     —*From a Declaration of Principles Jointly Adopted by a Committee of the American Bar Association and a Committee of Publishers and Associations*

McGraw-Hill books are available at special quantity discounts to use as premiums and sales promotions or for use in corporate training programs. To contact a representative, please e-mail us at bulksales@mcgraw-hill.com.

This book is printed on acid-free paper.

For My Mom

Contents

Acknowledgments

A MENTOR ONCE SAID TO ME, "NOTHING IS EVER REALLY ACCOMplished alone." These words were never truer than when it came to writing this book. I have so many wonderful colleagues, clients, and friends for whom I am grateful. Their wisdom, emotional support, and much needed laughter during the writing and publishing process was invaluable. I especially want to acknowledge:

My agent, Ken Lizotte, for believing in my book idea, finding a top-notch publisher, and supporting me even after the contract was signed. An agent who supports a writer during all phases of the process is rare, so thank you.

My acquisition editor, Jennifer Ashkenazy, for seeing the value of a book about affluent women for men, my editing manager, Jane Palmieri, and all the staff at McGraw-Hill who worked to make this book the best it could be.

The strong and powerful women in my life, who stand by me in good times and bad, and encourage me to dream big and celebrate both my small and large victories, especially Wendy Hanson, Fran Goldstein, Lauran Star, and Meridith Elliot Powell.

My past writing group partners, Susan Hammond and Stacey Shipman, for hanging in there with me when a publisher was nowhere on the horizon.

My male colleagues who, when called upon, offered the important male perspective and let me be (or at least think I was) "one of the guys," especially Tom Burke, Chris Bilello, and Jim Grubman, PhD.

The KBK Wealth Connection team for handling the details so I can focus on the big picture, especially Kelly Pelissier, Kathy Goughenour, Mary Hanley, Nicole Pillemer, and Tracy Pierce.

My independent study student from Bentley University who helped with this project, Rick Harkins.

The many wonderful women and men I interviewed for this book. Your openness to talk about a taboo subject and to share your insights into the advising and wealth management industry brought this book to life.

Lastly, I want to thank my husband Brian. Your faith in me and my ability to see projects through to the end—even when I can't see the end in sight—is a true gift that makes my life so much richer. Thanks for always loving me, for making me belly laugh every day, and for joining me on this adventure called life.

Introduction

FINANCIAL ADVISORS HAVE A BAD REPUTATION WITH WOMEN. MOST feel slighted by the industry and see it as catering only to male wealth creators. They resent the assumption that women are disinterested in financial matters, are not good with money, and "should not worry their pretty heads about it." They are dissatisfied customers, who have real economic power. And they are unhappy that the financial services industry does not provide products and services to meet their needs.

This dissatisfaction is not a new phenomenon. However, the financial crisis in 2008 and unethical advisors like Bernie Madoff certainly didn't make matters any better. While none of these factors are your fault individually, as a financial advisor working with high-net-worth clients you should be concerned. You have an uphill battle when it comes to attracting and connecting with female clients, and retaining them in your practice. And these women are getting wealthier by the day.

Over the next several decades women will inherit approximately $28.7 trillion in assets as a result of intergenerational wealth transfers.[1] Many of these women will become double inheritors, inheriting money from both parents and spouses. Others will accumulate wealth through their own professional and business accomplishments. In fact, women-owned businesses are growing at twice the national rate and account for 40 percent of privately held entities.[2] This growth is so rapid that one recent report by the Center for Women's Business Research claimed that "if U.S.-based women-owned businesses were their own country, they would have the fifth largest GDP in the world."[3] This statistic alone makes a strong argument for why you need to learn more about affluent female clients and how to stop underserving them.

There is one advantage to the financial advising industry historically underserving affluent female clients: it makes your task of becoming a sought-after financial advisor for wealthy women easier. Start by reading this book and investing the time it takes to increase your knowledge about women and wealth. Capitalize on what you already know, and add some new skills specifically designed for advising women. With a little practice, you can quickly become the advisor women talk about, refer to, and want for their friends.

How to Give Financial Advice to Women: Attracting and Retaining High-Net-Worth Female Clients is a book designed to give you an overview of female psychology and provide you with the skills you need to connect and communicate with affluent women in order to retain them in your practice. For the purposes of this book, I defined *affluent* as a person having $1 million or greater in investable assets. The book is packed with information about how women think and feel about money, life, and their financial advisors. Part I of the book, "Women and Wealth," teaches you the basics about the psychology of women and wealth. Topics include understanding the female brain and its impact on your advising style, the myths and realities of an affluent woman's life, her greatest concerns and how you can help, and the special needs of women going through various life transitions. By studying the emotional underpinning of the female experience, you will be better equipped to truly connect with women both individually and as a member of a couple.

Part II of the book, "Essential Skills for Advising Affluent Women," provides specific communication and advising techniques that are necessary to serve affluent female clients well. These skills include building trust, active listening, fostering financial confidence, working with women in couples, and preparing the client's children to receive wealth. This part ends with a chapter on how to market to affluent women and includes marketing dos and don'ts to make sure you are investing your time and resources wisely.

It is worth mentioning that *How to Give Financial Advice to Women* includes generalizations about male and female behaviors. Some facts are presented in a simplistic view to make a point or teach a concept. Please keep in mind that with any conversation about gender, some of the information may apply to your clients and some may not. For instance, while I am a woman writing about female clients, my thoughts and behaviors don't always conform to the gender research findings. I like to verbally spar with others; I am not patient or very nurturing when skiing with those new to the sport; and I don't like to cook, clean, or sew. It is easy to see that if an advisor made an assumption about me based on my gender, he would be incorrect and would potentially lose my business. Make sure you always view your female clients as individuals first and members of a gender second.

I have been asked frequently why I wrote a book on advising women for men. There are two reasons. First and foremost, I am passionate about empowering women. My entire career has been dedicated to inspiring them to feel better physically, emotionally, and financially. Over the years, I have witnessed too many women struggling with financial confidence, ignoring their financial lives, and fed up with the financial advisors they come into contact with. This book is written for them and all that they could not say to you. I want to stack the deck so that when a woman reaches out to the financial services industry, it is easy to locate a competent and caring female-friendly advisor.

The second reason I wrote this book is because I love coaching entrepreneurs. It is fun to share my expertise with financial advisors like you who are looking to build your book of business, who want to make a name for yourself in the industry, and who enjoy mastering the art of advising women. It is a great challenge to use my two decades of psychological training and consulting experience to reach out to advisors who are primarily male and inspire them to work with women. I have spent many weekends skiing and mountain biking with the boys and many weekdays listening to my female clients' stories. My hope is to share what I have learned from both genders to bridge the communication gap between affluent female women and their advisors.

I hope you enjoy and benefit from reading *How to Give Financial Advice to Women*. Like you, I am an entrepreneur who is always learning more about how to best serve my clients; therefore, I welcome your feedback. Please e-mail me at kbk@kbkwealthconnection.com with your thoughts on the book and how your female clients react to the tools and tips offered. Also feel free to check out my company's website at http://www.kbkwealthconnection.com. It is constantly being updated with articles, blogs, and other useful tools.

Until then, happy reading!
Kathleen

PART I

Women and Wealth

1

The Underserved Client

*People will forget what you said, they will forget
what you did, but they will never forget
how you made them feel.*

–Maya Angelou, American author and poet

OVER THE NEXT 40 YEARS, WOMEN ARE DUE TO INHERIT 70 PERCENT of the $41 trillion in intergenerational wealth transfers, or approximately $28.7 trillion in assets.[1] The first thing a woman is likely to do after receiving her inheritance is fire you. She will leave your firm and hire your competition not because of lack of investment performance or because you are not an expert in the field, but because she feels misunderstood, unheard, or overlooked.

Female clients need trustworthy, caring financial advisors like you. Women want advisors who provide sound financial advice to help them navigate life's ups and downs. Each client wants to know in her gut that you are on her side and that you understand how complicated it can be for her to care for herself while caring for others. She wants to be validated as an intelligent and competent person and feel like a client that you desire, not one you have to put up with. Overall, women simply want the same time, attention, and service you provide her male counterpart.

Unfortunately, this is not the experience for the majority of women. According to a State Farm Survey conducted in 2008, two-thirds of women don't trust financial service professionals.[2] More recently, the Boston Consulting Group surveyed 12,000 women from 21 countries for its *Global Inquiry into Women and Consumerism* study and discovered women are most dissatisfied with the financial services industry, of all industries, on both a service and product level.[3] These are startling statistics and provide strong evidence that the financial services industry has missed the mark with female clients.

This does not mean you have to continue this trend in your practice. In fact, it makes good business sense not to. Here are some facts you may not know:

♦ Women control the majority of personal wealth in the United States.[4]

♦ Women make approximately 80 percent of family household buying decisions, including those related to banking and financial services.[5]

♦ Of affluent women, 88 percent are moderately or highly involved in the oversight and management of their assets.[6]

♦ One in five firms with revenue of $1 million or more is woman owned.[7]

♦ The economic impact from women-owned businesses is $2.8 trillion annually.[8]

As the old Virginia Slim's cigarette commercial used to say, "You [women] have come a long way baby!"

Interestingly enough, the financial services industry is not the only one to historically overlook or discount the power of the female consumer: it has happened in the automobile, real estate, and technology industries as well. Progressive companies are scrambling to make up for past mistakes and win back or capture this important demographic. And based on just the few statistics above, you can see why.

Women are an important part of the client population and will continue to become more influential as time progresses. As a financial advisor, you can't afford not to learn how best to serve a woman and her family. She has the money and the decision-making power, whether she wears it on her sleeve or not.

The Opportunity: Female-Friendly Advisors

Women are looking for female-friendly advisors to work with now and in the future to help them receive, build, and pass on wealth. These advisors need to be knowledgeable, credentialed, and competent. They must possess communication and relationship-building skills specifically designed for working with female clients. In addition, they must understand a woman's need to build trust slowly, to be emotionally validated by her advisor, and to be able to share her story as part of the financial planning process.

Female-friendly advisors do not have to be women. In fact, many of them are not. Instead they are financial professionals who appreciate a woman's unique circumstances and the demands of being a wife, mother, daughter, friend, and professional. As Tom Burke, vice president of investments at South Shore Savings Bank, shares, "Women tend to be more 'advice receptive' than men. There tends to be a greater appreciation of the time invested on both sides to develop a basis for trust that goes beyond investment performance." Women are willing to take time to get to know you and work with you. But you have to be willing to invest the time as well.

Thirty percent or less of financial planning professionals are women.[9] Therefore, it is good news for male advisors (and their female clients) that this skill can be learned regardless of the gender of the advisor. And when done well, it will improve client satisfaction and retention ratings and help increase assets under management in the long run. Also, advising female clients can become a truly rewarding part of your job. As Burke puts it, "Meeting and developing relationships with many wonderful, powerful women is a reward I appreciate every day. Not to mention that working with women in transition has made a significant financial impact on my practice."

Not sure how to serve female clients well? Then you have picked up the right book because in the next several chapters, I will show you how.

IN HER OWN WORDS

My former financial advisor is a good example of a competent financial professional who failed to really listen and understand my needs as his female client. After the 2008 financial markets crashed, both my husband and I went to see this advisor. On the car ride over we decided how we wanted to handle our investments and talked about our respective feelings regarding the "loss." I waited the whole meeting to communicate this information to our advisor, but I never got a chance. He spent the whole meeting talking about the history of the stock market and how this was an anomaly. But he never asked me or my husband one question about how we felt about the value of our portfolio decreasing. He was too busy showing us how smart he was. After that meeting, I convinced my husband to fire him. I just can't work with someone who does not listen.

—*MARY, 39 YEARS OLD, MARRIED, CAREER PROFESSIONAL*

While female clients let go of financial advisors for a myriad of reasons, it usually boils down to one key factor—listening. Just like Mary did not feel heard by her advisor in their last meeting, many female clients complain that advisors don't listen and try to sell them products and services before they really get to know them.

Why the Financial Industry Missed the Mark

There are a few reasons why women have been overlooked by the financial advising industry for so long. First, the financial services industry was founded by men for men. Topics such as women and investing, women and wealth, and the value of female leadership in financial institutions have only entered the conversation in the last decade. It simply was not an industry focus. Second, women historically have not controlled wealth, earned money outside the home, or achieved equal financial footing with men. Financial advisors went after the individuals with the assets, and those individuals were not women. Last, many women suffer from a lack of financial confidence. Their silence at meetings, avoidance of financial discussions, and lack of investment and financial knowledge has been misinterpreted as not caring about money. Many women want to be more financially confident, but fear asking for help from financial advisors who use jargon and language that does not make sense to the average person.

It is ironic that financially savvy women feel pigeon-holed by the women and wealth movement and resent being lumped together with all women into one broad category, "women and money." As you can see, there is no one contributor and no easy solutions to serving affluent female clients better.

Men, Men, Men

The financial services industry was created by men to serve the male wealth creator; therefore, it is no wonder that women have felt left out. They were and still are. Approximately 80 percent of financial advisors, 90 percent of brokers, and 84 percent of financial corporate officers are men.[10] The industry's best practices, marketing strategies, selling tactics, and investing protocols were and still are developed primarily using a male's brain which thinks, acts, and behaves differently than the female's brain. In her bestselling book *The Female Brain*, Dr. Louann Brizendine shares that male and female brains are 99 percent the same, but the 1 percent gender difference in brain chemistry is evident in every cell of the body and it is what makes a man, a man and a woman, a woman.[11] It makes sense that if one gender is creating, developing, and selling financial services and products, then the end result would be heavily skewed toward that gender.

A good example is investment performance reporting. It is a common practice to share a client's return on investment for the year by comparing it to a standard benchmark such as the S&P 500 Index. The idea is that if you outperform this benchmark, you have done well and your advisor is a keeper. This approach to reporting is very male centric. Men like to compete and win, so if a male advisor lets the male client know that together they have beat the S&P, this makes both of their brains very happy.

However, for a female investor, this type of reporting may, and often does, fall flat. Her definition of success is not about winning and losing against the market, but instead is based on how well her portfolio performed in conjunction with her long-term life goals and objectives. He wants to win. She wants to survive and thrive. No one gender perspective is right or wrong, just different. And this difference has not yet been fully factored in with how the financial services industry does business and interacts with female clients.

In order for women to be better served by the industry, more women need to be involved in leadership roles, not to replace all the men, but to provide a much needed feminine balance to the leadership team. The industry, similar to many other fields, has a long way to go in bringing female executives and leaders to the table. Based on a report by *Treasury & Risk* in 2011, only 15 of the top 100 most influential people in finance are women.[12] But the tide is slowly turning as more women enter the field and more organizations such as the Women Advisors Forum, Barron's Top Women Advisors Summit, and others are offering educational and networking symposiums to support female professionals interested in becoming thought leaders in the industry.

Show Me the Money!

The second major factor resulting in women being underserved by the financial services industry is that for a long time they did not have money to invest. Historically, women were not property owners, and the primary method for women to gain access to any level of economic power was through marriage. A young woman's sole purpose was to fall in love, start a family, and be taken care of financially by a man for the rest of her life. You only need to look at fairy tales such as Cinderella and Sleeping Beauty to see how prominent this theme was (and unfortunately still is) for women.

While women were granted the right to own property in America in 1839, the legislative process was not completed nationally until the early twentieth century. By then women's wealth had increased, although they still did not have access to credit until the 1970s. Female investors entered the stock market in 1880, but were seen as "too impulsive and impressionable" to be on Wall Street.[13] The mindset at the time was that women should turn the management of their funds over to male advisors. While this mindset has changed over time, the fact that such a small fraction of financial advisors are women sends a very similar message to today's female client.

In the 1920s, some women entered the business world. This was the same time that women won the right to vote in the United States. But these women were anomalies and often seen as renegades in a time when the feminine ideal was to marry, stay at home, and raise a family. In 1930, 24 percent of women were gainfully employed outside the home, but in very traditional female occupations, such as teaching, nursing, and housekeeping.[14] This number jumped to 35 percent in the 1940s due to World War II and the need for more "manpower" to replace the men who had enlisted to fight in the war.[15]

The real shift in women becoming wealth creators in their own right began in 1970 with the Women's Rights Movement. This was the first time women were entering the workforce in larger numbers and becoming millionaires in their own right. The work-life dilemma was born out of the desire to be a female professional earning her own money, yet still wanting to be a perfect wife and mother. By 1990, it was commonplace for women to have careers, but pay inequity resulted in them earning less than men and accumulating assets at a slower pace. They were still viewed as those who supplemented the household income, not as the creator of wealth.

IN HER OWN WORDS

I would love to have my financial advisor give me the same level of attention that he gives to my husband. I am the primary breadwinner, but when the advisor calls, he talks with my husband. He only e-mails my husband. He has golf outings for his clients—my husband loves those, but I don't golf. I'd like to be treated as equal but different. In other words, give me the same level of attention, but customize it to my unique needs as a woman.

—KATHY, 55 YEARS OLD, MARRIED BUSINESSWOMAN AND GRANDMOTHER OF SIX

Currently, women still struggle to earn equal pay, but more and more females are starting businesses, accumulating assets, and investing in the market with the purpose of building wealth. In 2010, women finally tipped the balance by taking control of over 50 percent of the personal wealth in this country.[16] In just 100 years, women have gone from being unwelcome on Wall Street to being important players in business and wealth generation. While female entrepreneurs still have to fight to get access to capital, they are no longer allowing men to make all the financial decisions for them. This trend in women creating, controlling, and managing wealth is only going to continue to grow.

Lack of Financial Confidence

The last factor in women being overlooked by the financial services industry is their collectively low financial confidence. According to a 2006 study conducted by Allianz Life Insurance on women, money, and power, 90 percent of the 1,925 women respondents ages 21 to over 60 reported feeling insecure when it comes to personal finance.[17] Many women also lag behind men when it comes to financial knowledge.[18] Of course there are many exceptions to these statistics; however, this overall lack of financial mastery has resulted in many women being their own worst enemy when it comes to demanding that the financial services industry make reforms to better meet their needs as clients.

Working as a wealth psychology coach and consultant, I have heard the same story time and time again from my female clients. "I don't know enough to see an advisor," many of them declare. This type of thinking is why women do not engage with financial advisors, attend annual review meetings with their partners and families, or take an active role in their financial lives. It keeps women behind the financial eight ball.

The flip side of this issue is that many financial advisors assume and perpetuate the myth that women are not interested in financial matters. Just because a woman's financial confidence is low does not mean she is not concerned. Furthermore, some women are very self-assured in the financial arena, but they are tired of being mislabeled as inexperienced or not interested because they are females. When asked about engaging more women in the financial advising process, many advisors say, "Why bother pursuing her as a client or engaging her as a member of a couple? She just doesn't care." I would argue that she cares, but feels as if the industry does not care about her.

Women are interested in taking care of themselves financially. But they are not interested in seminars or meetings that are geared solely toward a male audience. Women want workshops and meetings that

In Her Own Words

I manage my own financial affairs. In past experiences I have had male advisors disregard my opinion and concerns. I stopped asking for help and educated myself.

—JESSIE, 52-YEAR-OLD PROFESSIONAL, MARRIED WITH THREE CHILDREN

allow for plenty of dialogue, time to talk with other participants about their concerns and get information on how to better take care of their wealth so they can take care of their loved ones. These women are hungry to have an impact in the business world, to raise financially astute daughters (and sons), and to give back to their community.

Make sure you don't confuse lack of confidence with disinterest. It really just boils down to women needing and wanting to learn differently, to feel included and valued in advisor-client relationships, and to be comfortable and able to engage an advisor no matter what their level of financial literacy.

Summary

Many financial services institutions and advisors are taking action through women initiatives to better serve affluent female clients. While some firms have made a real effort to change corporate culture and the products and services offered to women of wealth, many others have just given it lip service. Believe me, women know the difference. Women thrive on connection, authenticity, and partnership. If you offer all three to your female clients, you are bound to become a trusted advisor in their eyes.

Female clients have money to invest and are inheriting and creating more financial resources daily. Their economic power is growing, and those in the financial services industry that are responding will reap the rewards. A woman makes the majority of the buying decisions, including if she and her husband are going to hire you. So isn't it time that you make the effort to really get to know her?

Your Next Step: Your Female-Friendly Quotient (FFQ)

How female friendly is your current advising practice? Find out by circling "True" or "False" below. To get an accurate assessment, mark your responses according to your current practice, not based on what you think is the right answer. At the end, find out how to score this assessment to reveal your Female-Friendly Quotient (FFQ).

1. My practice is at a minimum equally weighted in terms of female versus male clients. (Only include clients you are actively working with either individually or as a member of a couple.)   True   False

2. Women face a variety of financial hurdles that are different than what men face.   True   False

3. When I meet with prospects, I need to know if they are going to sign up for my services within the first two appointments; otherwise, I am wasting my time.   True   False

4. I offer educational forums and client events specifically for women.   True   False

5. When I communicate with my female clients, I find it important to stress my expertise so that they feel comfortable working with me.   True   False

6. All women prefer to work with female advisors; therefore, I refer most women clients to my female colleagues.   True   False

7. When I am advising a couple, I communicate with the partner who speaks up the most.   True   False

8. I adjust my communication style to meet the preferred style of my client.   True   False

9. When I am advising a couple, I check in with both partners each time I have a question.   True   False

10. I offer individual meetings for my female clients who are members of a couple.   True   False

11. I communicate with other members of a client's financial team, such as their accountant, banker, and estate attorney, regularly.   True   False

12. If a female client is not talking, she is not learning.   True   False

13. During a client annual review, I spend a fair amount of time talking about investment performance relative to benchmarks such as the S&P.   True   False

14. I find it important to tie investment performance results to real-life events for my female clients.   True   False

15. When I develop a financial plan, I make sure the client articulates clearly her family values, life goals, and wishes for the next generation.   True   False

16. I offer intergenerational wealth services as part of my practice.   True   False

17. I avoid talking about emotional issues related to money with my clients.   True   False

18. I am open to and/or work with family wealth consultants, family therapists, and other consultants to help my female clients manage and pass on their wealth.   True   False

19. I do not offer financial literacy resources or training to my clients as I don't see this as part of my job.   True   False

20. The majority of women view wealth the same as men, i.e., as a means to power and control.   True   False

Your score: Give yourself 2 points for each of the following answers and then add up the total points to find out your FFQ.

1. True	6. False	11. True	16. True
2. True	7. False	12. False	17. False
3. False	8. True	13. False	18. True
4. True	9. True	14. True	19. False
5. False	10. True	15. True	20. False

FFQ Range

36–40 Points:	Congratulations! You are a very female-friendly advisor.
22–34 Points:	Nice job. You have a little work to do, but you are well on your way to being a female-friendly advisor.
0–20 Points:	You have some work to do, but you can raise your FFQ simply by reading this book and completing each of the *Your Next Action* coaching exercises at the end of each chapter.

The Psychology of Women and Wealth

The great question that has never been answered and which I have not yet been able to answer, despite my thirty years of research into the feminine soul, is "What does a woman want?"

—Sigmund Freud, founder of psychoanalysis

WOMEN WANT RESPECT FROM THE FINANCIAL SERVICES INDUSTRY. They want to be heard and appreciated and know that their financial advisors are genuinely interested in working with them. Women want advisors who are concerned about their well-being, their family's financial health, and their nonfinancial lives. They want to feel welcome at financial meetings and treated as partners in the financial planning and investment process.

Unfortunately, many advisors do not invest time and energy in understanding the psychology of women and wealth and how to best serve this demographic. Assumptions are made that female clients perceive the world, money, and relationships similarly to the way men do. This misconception leads advisors to miss the boat when prospecting and advising women. The traditional transaction business model commonly used in financial services does not meet a woman's social or neurological need for connection. Instead, a woman wants an ongoing coaching relationship with her financial advisor. She wants a professional who understands her first and sells to her second.

IN HER OWN WORDS

I find men in the financial world don't understand me. They appear to talk down to me as if I don't understand my own finances. Women today not only spend more, we are also making more and we are the CEOs of the household finances. You want my business, then you have to understand me first.

—*LAURAN, 43-YEAR-OLD MARRIED MOTHER OF THREE, BUSINESS OWNER*

The good news is that the industry is slowly changing to be more client centered. The financial crisis in 2008 led many clients to become more demanding and savvy when it comes to working with financial advisors. While this can be challenging for you, the advisor, it also has a silver lining. It is forcing the industry and firms to be more client oriented in their marketing, products, and delivery methods. This shift in the industry is a perfect fit for women because they love to be understood, known, and appreciated for their complexities. Female clients crave authentic advisors who happen to be experts. They want you to be willing to go in the trenches with them, to celebrate their victories, and to comfort them during life's setbacks. Women want a relationship with their advisors and will fire those who don't have the interest, time, or skills to engage in ongoing working partnerships.

There is no magic formula for connecting with affluent women, but having good chemistry certainly helps. Good chemistry is measured in terms of excellent communicating, listening, and interpersonal skills. It is based more on intuition than rational thought. It is the feeling you get when you meet someone for the first time and just click.

Be careful in assuming you have good chemistry with a female client. Often advisors, especially male advisors, are overly confident in their relationships with their female clients. Many women remain silent unless asked about the quality of the relationship and bide their time until they have control of the assets. If they don't feel a connection with you, they silently wait it out, sometimes in an effort to respect their husband's wishes, and then transfer their assets to the competition when their husband or partner is no longer in the picture. It is a startling and eye-opening fact that 70 percent of female widows fire their financial advisors within one year of the death of their spouses.[1] It is crucial that you don't wait to develop and nurture a personal relationship with each of your female clients, whether she is single or a member of a couple. Otherwise, it may be too late.

Being able to see the world through your client's eyes is a key part of good chemistry. Investing time and resources in learning about affluent women and their life experiences, both collectively and individually, is vital to authentically connecting with this demographic and building trust. As an advisor, you need to appreciate the pressures and rewards inherent in being a woman of wealth in our culture. You need to comprehend how the female brain works and how it is different than the male brain. You need to understand gender differences while still treating every female client as a unique individual. If you have good chemistry with your female clients and a keen understanding of the psychology of women and wealth, you will upstage your competition when it comes to connecting and retaining your affluent female clients.

It is important to note that good chemistry with a client is gender neutral. You can be a male advisor and connect very well with women clients. Or you can be a female advisor and not click with other women. Contrary to popular belief in the advising world, gender is not a guarantee when prospecting and selling to women. In fact, women advisors need to be careful not to make an assumption that they have the competitive advantage just because of their sex. When they do make that mistake, these female advisors spend too much time being friendly and not enough time communicating their value as an expert who can help. So don't tell yourself you can't compete with female colleagues when it comes to connecting and working with affluent women, because it simply is not true.

I'll bet you're thinking right now, "But the women I meet and work with are not interested in meeting with me!" Yes, there are some women who are not interested in your services and do not want to participate in actively managing their finances. Some are traditionalists and believe it is the man's job to make and manage the money. Others stick their heads in the sand and refuse to take adult responsibility when it comes to their finances. But many, many more are concerned about money and investing and want to be part of the financial planning and management process. No matter what you think of Suze Orman, her fast rise to fame highlights how hungry women are for financial advice and services that cater to them. So the next time a wife, daughter, or female partner ops out of a meeting with you, don't shake your head and say, "See, she is not interested." Instead ask yourself, "What can I do differently to engage her in the advisor-client relationship, and how can I communicate to her that she is a valuable part of her family's financial team?"

The Female Experience

According to Bridget Brennan, author of *Why She Buys: The New Strategy for Reaching the World's Most Powerful Consumers*, "Gender is the most powerful determinant of how a person views the world and everything in it. It is more powerful than age, income, race, or geography." A female's experience is unique compared to a man's in that she is socialized differently from the time she is born. Baby girls are dressed in pink and told they are cute and nice like sugar and spice. Boys are outfitted in blue and praised for being rugged, tough little men. Young girls have tea parties; young boys play in the dirt and race Matchbox cars. Young women grow up and know that looking good, getting married, and starting a family is how society defines female success. Boys grow up knowing that making money, competing for the corner office, and being a good provider is the key to masculinity. While family upbringing and personal temperament influence how loudly each of us answers this societal call, these powerful messages impact our collective psyche, our interpersonal style, and our worldview.

As a wealth psychology consultant specializing in women and wealth, I live and work in both male- and female-dominated cultures. I love the diversity, and shift back and forth between worlds pretty effortlessly. However, a few years back I was really struck by the juxtaposition of these two worlds after attending one women's conference and one all-male networking lunch back-to-back. While reflecting on these two experiences, I realized how much I unconsciously shift my communication style to fit my audience. For example, at the women's conference I spoke about how women can earn more in the business world. I shared a story about my struggle to make more money as a career professional and the fear I had that I would be seen as an overly aggressive and money-hungry witch. The female audience laughed, nodded in agreement, and shared their concerns about asking for money with the larger group. These businesswomen understood my plight as a female in the working world trying to get ahead, trying to be seen as feminine and uncertain how to negotiate for more money in a man's world.

The next day, I attended an all-male luncheon at a private country club. While all the businessmen were nice and polite, I clearly was not "in Kansas" anymore. Instead of sharing my feelings, I told this group a story about a recent mountain bike ride where I took a header jumping over a log. I bragged about how I got up, still bleeding, jumped back on the bike, and managed to finish ahead of two of the guys. The men laughed and understood innately what it was like to be knocked down, heckled by their friends, and then to push through injuries to make it to the finish line. Because this is what men do—they compete. While I still was the only girl at the table, I earned respect with one simple story. If I could hang with the guys and "win," I was okay.

These two events highlight the variances between societal expectations based on gender. The female culture is one of connection, shared emotional experiences, and support. The male culture is one of competition, shared physical activities, and one-upsmanship. Neither one is right or wrong, just different. If I shared my mountain bike story with my female audience, many of them would have thought I was crazy to get dirty and beat up riding a bike. The same holds true if I had shared my vulnerability and mixed feelings story with the men.

The dilemma that many financial advisors face when working with female clients is that the rules of the road are unfamiliar. How relationships are formed and the expectations inherent in partnerships are altered. If you take a male culture approach to connecting and advising female clients, you are likely to lose those clients pretty quickly. As Ann Hughes, the founder of The Female Affect, states, "We need to do a better job of meeting their needs and making them feel at home in this industry by doing business in a way females want to have business done." She goes on to say that while the industry has not been successful in this mission, it is not a complicated process. It simply involves raising the comfort level of all advisors, male and female, in connecting with and working with affluent women.

When women entered the workforce in the 1960s, 1970s, and 1980s, they needed to learn and adapt to how men did business. Any successful businesswoman, especially one working in a male-dominated industry such as financial services, had to figure out

---

IN HER OWN WORDS

Understand that the ways in which we perceive our worlds are different, more broadly and more emotionally perhaps, than from a man's point of view. Information may need to be delivered differently.

—SUSAN, 56-YEAR-OLD DIVORCED MOTHER OF THREE CHILDREN

---

pretty quickly how to navigate successfully in a man's world. While the men I work with refuse to show me the "men's handbook," stating they were sworn to secrecy at birth, I do know enough about men to know you don't talk too much about feelings—you bond by engaging in sports and you never, ever let anyone see you cry.

So what are the rules of the road for navigating the female world? There are many, and they are complicated. But here are six guidelines to help you start to better understand and feel more comfortable in the world of women.

Rule 1. Women need to tell their story. To be effective attracting, connecting, and advising a woman, you need to listen to and understand her experience. You can do this by carefully listening, by asking curious, open-ended questions, and by doing your best to put yourself in her shoes. Not only is she socialized to share, she gets a biological boost in doing so as the pleasure centers in her brain light up when she does.

Rule 2. Women get personal quickly. The best way to observe this phenomenon is to set up a network appointment with a female and a male colleague for the same day. Notice how much time he spends proving his expertise and how much time she uses to talk about what you two have in common. Often in sharing your similarities, she will initiate a conversation about family, friends, and life challenges.

Rule 3. Women communicate using feeling words. Now don't fret if you are a male advisor and think you simply can't or don't want to discuss feelings. She will do most of the talking and emoting; you just need to listen, validate her feelings, and show empathy. Why do women do this? Because women connect through discussing their vulnerabilities and not through sharing activities the way men typically do. For example, if I kayak with a girlfriend, we share secrets and insecurities while paddling. With a male companion, we talk about the tide and the wind, and challenge each other to a paddle-off.

Rule 4. Women define success as being "indispensable." Women love to help and be seen as the go-to person for assistance. Men typically prefer to be independent and define success in terms of doing it alone. Make sure you highlight how a female client is a valuable and an indispensable part of the financial planning team because it is important in the female world for her to be seen as helpful.

Rule 5. Women remember details and read body language. Women excel at reading facial expressions and body language, and remembering details. Some people surmise that this is due to a woman's natural instincts as a mother. She is wired to read facial and body cues and to respond quickly to make sure her newborn baby remains safe. Whatever the reason, making eye contact, communicating interest through nonverbal communication, and paying attention to details are very important in the female culture. A male client might not care if you follow up after each meeting with a note to say thank you, but doing so with a woman may mean the difference between keeping a client and losing one. Trust me, details matter.

Rule 6. Women are loyal. Once trust is established, women are extremely loyal friends, lovers, employees, and clients. Because being in relationships is what defines them and brings them pleasure, women work diligently to establish, maintain, and preserve their personal and professional relationships. This loyalty is why women refer more

IN HER OWN WORDS

Look me in the eye when you talk to me, even if my husband is in the room. My opinion matters and I want to feel like you understand that it does.

—LYNN, A 56-YEAR-OLD MARRIED CAREER PROFESSIONAL

friends, family members, and colleagues to financial advisors than men do. According to Delia Passi, author of *Winning the Toughest Customer: The Essential Guide to Selling to Women*, a female client is likely to refer to a financial advisor 26 times in her lifetime, whereas a man is likely to refer to a financial advisor only 11 times in his lifetime.[2] Women are less likely to blame financial advisors for poor portfolio performance than male clients are. Men tend to be overly confident and have unrealistic expectations for their advisors, often blaming them for portfolio losses even during a down market. Women take on too much responsibility for investment performance and internalize guilt and shame over financial losses, even when advisors lead them astray. This behavior can be detrimental to their financial health because they are likely to stay with advisors who do not meet their needs longer than men would. Even highly intelligent, assertive women find breaking up with financial advisors hard to do.

Don't worry about knowing all the rules of the feminine world. These six rules will get you off to a good start. Take the time to ask your clients to tell you more about the rules of the feminine world. By being curious about their world, your clients will feel appreciated and cared for, and they will know you are truly interested in them as people, not just assets. In the male-dominated world, asking questions and not knowing may be perceived as a weakness or vulnerability. However, in the world according to women, it is a sign of strength. Asking questions and listening to the answers builds trust and communicates that her expertise and wisdom is a valuable part of the financial advising equation.

Female Development

It may be surprising for you to learn that relatively little was known about the psychology of women and female development until the 1980s. Today, it is widely understood that women are more relationship and feelings oriented. However, it was only three decades ago when research validated this fact. Prior to that time, a false assumption was made by psychologists that human development was identical for both genders. Research studies were conducted using only male subjects and the conclusions that were drawn were generalized to women. Ironically, the field of psychology made the same error that is currently being made by the financial services industry: it assumed that men and women want, need, and value the same things in relationships and life.

A psychologist named Carol Gilligan changed the world's understanding of what it meant to be a woman when she wrote her groundbreaking book, *In a Different Voice*. This work marked the first time the human behavior of women was studied separately from men's. She observed and subsequently wrote that women are relational and have a need for connection with others. She discovered that women find self-worth by creating and maintaining relationships, and care deeply about helping family, friends, and the community.[3] This was exactly the opposite of how men develop over time. Men are more individualized as they gain self-esteem through completing tasks independently and by competing. While some men like to help, it does not define who they are and their value to the same extent as it does for women. As a result of this work, behaviors and interpersonal styles that were previously viewed as weak and neurotic are now seen as signs of healthy female development.

Gilligan's work was enlightening and comforting for many women who felt misunderstood and mistreated by society. Denise P. Federer, PhD, a licensed psychologist specializing in family wealth consulting and founder of the Federer Performance Management Group, explains how Gilligan's work and relational theory impacted her meetings with couples and families. "This work really crystallized how men and women communicate differently and how this is a source of miscommunication between the sexes. I had always witnessed it in my office, but now I had a theory to back it up."

A woman's desire to care for others makes her a perfect fit for the role of caregiver. Sociologists believe the high importance women place on getting along with others began as a survival strategy back in primitive times. While men went off to hunt for food, women were left by the campfire to take care of the children and to work with the other members of the community. If for some reason a woman's male partner did not return from a hunting trip, the fate of her and her family was directly impacted by how well she got along and related to others. Of course, in modern times, community connections are not a matter of life or death, but for some women it can still feel that way. The fear of disconnection contributes to women not negotiating better compensation, staying in bad marriages, and not telling financial advisors they are dissatisfied with the service. It explains the female tendency to put children, parents, romantic partners, bosses, coworkers, employees, girlfriends, and virtually everyone else first. And while many women from more recent generations have the benefit of being raised by parents who modeled that women can compete and excel individually, there is still a strong societal expectation (and now biological evidence) for women to be peacekeepers and caretakers.

Now let's turn our attention from the societal influences on a woman's experience and development to some neurological influences.

The Female Brain

Many of the relational psychology theories offered by Gilligan and her colleagues can now be further supported by advances in the field of neuroscience. Gender preferences relative to communication and interpersonal styles can be accounted for and understood relative to how the male and female brains differ in size and structure. In the national bestselling book *The Female Brain*, Louann Brizendine, MD, states, "There is no unisex brain. She was born with a female brain that came complete with its own impulses. Girls arrive already wired as girls, and boys arrive already wired as boys. Their brains are different by the time they're born, and their brains are what drive their impulses, values, and their reality."[4]

Advances in neuroscience offer further explanation for why gender differences exist in our clients and in our society. You only need to look to classic and popular sitcoms like *All in the Family*, *The Cosby Show*, and *Modern Family* to see how men and women act and react to life in often conflicting and comical ways. These gender inconsistencies can lead to frustration and conflict or, when understood, to clarity and acceptance. Your job as a financial advisor is not to become a brain scientist, but to use the research about the female brain to assist you in responsibly and effectively advising affluent women in your practice. This research becomes even more paramount to your success with female clients if you, in fact, have a male brain.

Let's start with a very basic overview of the human brain. Our brains are made up of different sections, with each part controlling and regulating the body's various functions. There are two sides to the brain, commonly referred to as the *right* and *left hemispheres*. Ironically, the right brain controls the left side of the body and is responsible for creativity and artistic abilities, and the left brain controls the right side of the body and is responsible for logic and analytical thinking. If someone refers to you as left-brained, chances are you are good with numbers, statistics, and analytics, and this may be why you decided on a career in finance. If you are more right-brained, you may excel at relationships and creative endeavors. Often advisors with right-brain dominance entered the field of financial services primarily to help people, and these advisors prefer to let others look at data.

In Jason Zweig's book *Your Money and Your Brain: How the New Science of Neuroeconomics Can Help Make You Rich*, he offers another way to look at the brain and its functioning. He uses the terms *reflective* and *reflexive thinking* rather than referring to right and left hemispheres. According to Zweig, reflective thinking largely resides in the prefrontal cortex, or the CEO of the brain. This type of thinking is used to solve complex problems and make long-term plans. Reflexive thinking is located in the cerebral cortex and plays a central role in identifying and recognizing rewards, such as food, sex, or money. It also reacts to real or perceived danger. The reflexive system reacts instinctively and emotionally, whereas the reflective system ponders, contemplates, then decides. It is a dilemma for clients (and advisors) because financial decisions are often made using the reflexive brain, not the reflective brain.[5] This is why smart people make stupid financial decisions, especially when under real or perceived stress. It is not that they are less intelligent, it is just that the part of the brain called into action is more emotional, reactive, and protective and less capable of rational thought than when they are not "under siege."

All human brains have reflective and reflexive thinking. However, the way the female brain is structured makes women more relationship oriented than men. This explains why women put relationships first and foremost in most situations and men feel less of a need to connect. It also helps us understand why women tend to be more focused than men on caregiving, passing on money and life values to the next generation, and using wealth to better the community as a whole.

Below are three areas of the brain and how each is structured differently in the female versus the male brain:

◆ **Amygdala and limbic system.** The amygdala is the center for emotion, fear, and aggression. It is located in the limbic system and is the part of the brain responsible for the fight or flight response. When faced with danger, humans react in one of two ways; anger and fighting (fight response) or panic and fleeing (flight response). This explains why a dramatic drop in the stock market prices causes some clients to lash out at you in anger and others to disappear from your radar completely.

   The female brain's limbic system is typically larger than the male's. Scientists hypothesize that the larger limbic system contributes to women being more compelled to care for others, even at their own personal and financial expense.

◆ **Hippocampus.** The hub of emotion and memory formation is called the *hippocampus*. This section of the brain is larger in women than men and accounts for a woman's ability to remember specific details. For example, a woman is more likely to remember tiny details of an emotional fight, whereas men may not even remember having the confrontation. This trait often drives men crazy because they don't possess the same superpower. The larger hippocampus also could contribute to some women wanting their financial advisors to remember personal details about their life. They view this type of remembering as a form of caring.

◆ **Corpus callosum.** This part of the brain transmits signals and connects the left and the right side of the brain. Women have more connections between the left and right hemispheres, making them excellent at multitasking and verbal communication. The male brain has more limited connection between hemispheres, resulting in men being less verbal and more single-task focused. This part of a woman's hard-wiring may explain why she has trouble understanding how a man can come home from work, see dishes in the sink, and not wash them. Misconceived as not caring, men, because of their male brain, may fixate on reading the paper; therefore, the dishes don't get picked up on their radar.

Because the female brain is wired to be more verbal, a financial advisor would be wise to allow time in each meeting for a female client to tell her story. By verbally sharing details and talking through her choices, she is working toward a financial decision. Interestingly enough, scans of the female brain show that when she is bonding with others, the pleasure centers of her brain light up. The same is not true for the male brain.

Advances in the field of neurology offer valuable insights into your female client's mind. She is typically highly verbal, able to juggle multiple tasks, and likely to notice and care about small details. For instance, a lack of family photos on your desk may not raise a red flag for a male client, but this minutia is likely to be picked up by a woman and possibly questioned. A female client may need to tell you her personal story as part of the trust-building process in a way that men typically do not need to do. Women may emote more when sharing stories, but this does not mean they are weak and fragile, just that they have greater access to their emotions than most men do. And lastly, if a woman is a member of a couple, she may outwardly appear bored because she is sitting in the meeting silently, but instead she may be just listening, waiting for her cue to chime in.

While the field of neuroscience is still in its infancy, these brain variances are interesting and useful in working with clients. If you have a male brain, it is important to remember how you process information, and how you view the world may be very different than how your female clients do. If you are a female advisor, you need to be careful not to overgeneralize your experience to all women. Remember brain science can inform your work with clients, but it should not take the place of curious, open-ended questioning and exploration about your client's unique goals, values, and preferences.

Women and Wealth

Women are socialized and hardwired differently than men, and their view of money and wealth is different too. When surveyed, 54 percent of women associated wealth with the word *security*, whereas men typically associate wealth with words such as *status* and *power*.[6] Women want security for their family and friends, and for future generations. They want to use their wealth to be independent and to have the freedom to make choices about how they live. In general, affluent women want to use their wealth to make the world a better place for their children, grandchildren, and great-grandchildren. And after their loved ones are taken care of, they want to devote time and resources to causes near to their hearts and to philanthropy to support the community.

Despite viewing wealth as a source of security, women often put their long-term financial health at risk by putting others' needs ahead of their own. Time and time again, I hear intelligent and accomplished women tell me they are saving for their children's college educations and not putting money away for retirement. On the surface, this fits with the societal expectation of women being caregivers first and individuals second. The problem is there are col-

---

IN HER OWN WORDS

Listen to me and answer my questions. Do not assume you have a clue about my life, how I operate, and what I need. And if you don't first ask me how my kids are doing, you've already lost the sale and the relationship.

—MARCIA, 50-YEAR-OLD SMALL-BUSINESS OWNER AND MOTHER OF TWO

lege scholarships and loans available for children to attend school, but no scholarships or loans for retirement. Despite women living longer and earning less than men, they are typically more risk averse and, therefore, often underfund their retirement accounts. In general, women worry more about money than men do. One study states that 30 percent of women, compared to only 17 percent of men, had high levels of anxiety about finances.[7] The researchers attributed these findings to "women's greater sense of obligation to children and the home." All in all, women have a lot of work to do in this area, and you are in a great position to help.

The gift of being a female is that she deeply cares about others; the curse is that she often puts others first at her own expense. Caregiving for elderly parents is a prime example. According to a study by the National Alliance of Caregiving, 66 percent of all caregivers are women.[8] Another study conducted by Met Life revealed that, on average, a woman loses $324,044 in income due to caring for children, parents, and friends.[9] This is a result of more women taking time off from their professional careers and missing out on large amounts of potential income that could be invested for wealth accumulation and retirement purposes. These women also forgo promotions, matching 401(k) plans, and learning opportunities that would keep them competitive in the marketplace.

Caregivers are also at a higher risk for developing health problems, such as lower immune system functioning, increased depression and anxiety, and in some cases, the use and abuse of food, drugs, and alcohol. While most women would not trade the opportunity to stay at home with their children or take care of an ill parent, there certainly is a high financial and emotional price to pay.

A female-friendly financial advisor needs to be aware of a woman's definition of wealth, her commitment to caregiving, and her need to plan for these unique female financial dilemmas over the course of her life. The failure to adequately save for retirement and unexpected events, such as illness, death of a spouse, or divorce, is exactly why many women need a competent and caring financial advisor like you. Don't buy into the myth that if a woman is well off today, she is all set for the future. One unfortunate turn of events and she might not be. Your job is to coach her on how to balance her family's needs with her own because she may have trouble putting herself first.

Myth Busting

There are several myths about women and wealth. These myths perpetuate misconceptions about women and money, and turn female clients off. You need to be aware of these myths and do your part in setting the record straight with your current clients and your colleagues.

Below are the top five myths about women and money and some facts to help you bust them wide open.

Myth 1. Women are not good at math. In 1992, Mattel released a talking Barbie Doll that uttered the words, "Math is tough." This doll was promptly attacked by the American Association of University Women for perpetuating the myth that girls were less proficient at math and science than boys.[10] Over a decade later in 2005, Lawrence H. Summers, the then president of Harvard University, made a controversial statement at an academic conference suggesting that there was an innate difference between the sexes that caused fewer women to succeed in math and science careers than men. His controversial comments were splashed all over the media, and a year later, Summers resigned.[11]

Both these events speak to how ingrained the belief is that women are not good with numbers. However, research disproves this fallacy. One interesting study out of the University of California, San Diego, reported nurture not nature accounts for the gap in math skills. The researchers compared two rural tribes in India. The first tribe did not allow women to own land or attend school for as long as men did; the second allowed both sexes to own land and attend school for an equal amount of time. In the tribe with equal rights, women were equally proficient in math skills as the men. In the male-dominated tribe, men outperformed the women in this area. The researchers concluded that environment, not gender, determines a person's math abilities.[12]

There is a growing movement to expose more women to learning and mentoring opportunities in the fields of math, engineering, finance, and science. Time will tell if this exposure increases the number of females entering these professions. But either way, it is important to know that girls can do math and are just as good with numbers as boys.

Myth 2. Women are impulsive spenders. Most, if not all, of the media coverage on overspending tells the same tale of a lonely, wealthy woman at the mall buying clothes and shoes she will never wear. Despite this image, overshopping is an equal opportunity problem. According to April Lane Benson, PhD, a nationally known psychologist who specializes in the treatment of compulsive buying disorder and author of the book *To Buy or Not to Buy: Why We Overshop and How to Stop*, "Money is an equal-opportunity, all-purpose mood changer." She has discovered that just as many men impulsively spend and overshop as women, although men generally adopt a work frame and women a leisure frame to the activity. "One major difference is how society labels it. Women overshop; men collect, a term that gives the activity a highbrow, slightly refined cast. But the underlying impulsive behavior is the same."

Overspending is a behavior used, often unconsciously, as a coping strategy for difficult feelings such as anxiety, depression, and low self-worth. While women are statistically more prone to suffer from anxiety and depression than men, our consumer-driven society is fertile ground for any individual, regardless of gender, to shop and acquire material possessions to temporarily boost self-esteem, cover up insecurities, and distract oneself from life's struggles. Because women make 80 percent of the household purchases in this country, she is more likely to be seen as the impulsive shopper because she shops more.[13] But you only need to look at history for some wonderful examples of men with the same problem. The first president of the United States, George Washington, was a classic compulsive shopper and more recently, Michael Jackson, the King of Pop, died with millions of dollars of debt due to his overspending habits.[14] So remember, anyone can impulsively shop.

Myth 3. Women are too emotional to invest wisely. This myth began in 1817 when the New York Stock Exchange came into existence and banned women from participating in trading activities. It was not until 63 years later in 1880 that women got involved in the market, much to the chagrin of the male brokers.[15] In the book *Women and Their Money 1700–1950: Essays on Women and Finance*, a story is told of a trader named Henry Clews. He claimed Wall Street should be off limits to women since they were too impulsive and impressionable. He went further to say women should turn over the management of their funds to male advisors. Time and behavioral finance proved Clews wrong. Several behavioral research studies have found women investors to outperform men in the long term.[16] The reason is men try to compete with the market and chase returns, leading to more frequent trading and high transaction costs. Conversely, women take a long time to make an initial investment decision, but once they do, they are committed for the long run. Women are less reactive to short-term changes in the market, trade less frequently than men, and realize better long-term investment performance as a result.

Myth 4. Women would rather let men manage the family finances. Women are the chief financial officers of their households in 66 out of 100 homes, according to the 2010 Women and Affluence Study by Women & Co.[17] This trend is on the rise; in 2008, the percentage was 63 percent. This number rose to 88 percent with increased wealth, and women in the ultra-high net worth market reported they play a high to moderate role in the management of the family's assets.[18] And when it comes to retirement, 90 percent of women participate in decisions that affect their household's retirement and investment accounts.[19] The truth is women want to be involved, and many more are actively involved in managing family finances.

Myth 5. Women are not interested in wealth management. Historically, wealth management has been a boys' club. However, the gender gap in finance is shrinking as more women enter the field. The Bureau of Labor reported in 2010 that 31 percent of personal financial advisors were women.[20] Advising clients lends itself to a woman's strengths in relationship building and communication, allowing some of these female advisors to outperform the men. Organizations such as Directions for Women, The Female Affect, and Women Advisors Forum are offering forums and networking opportunities to facilitate the advancement of women in financial services. When I speak at these forums and organizations, I see how women can and are interested in wealth management and are working hard to level the playing field going forward.

As you can see, women are good at math; are not too emotional to spend, invest, and manage money; and want to be players in the field of financial services and wealth management. Female clients are especially intuitive and good at detecting those financial advisors who give the advancement of women lip service versus those who really believe in equality for women. Be part of the group of advisors who educates clients and colleagues about the facts about women and money and dispels the myths. Believe me, she will notice.

Summary

If you want to be a female-friendly advisor and attract and retain more affluent women in your practice, you need to learn and appreciate gender differences. These include an understanding of how it feels to be raised a woman in our society as well as how the female brain is wired. The psychological and physiological need for connection and harmony makes relationships with female clients at times complicated, but also rich and rewarding. Take the time to connect with your current female clients and search out new ones. The time and energy you invest will pay big dividends as she will be loyal, refer her family and friends, and often be a joy to work with.

While some in the financial services industry prefer to treat all clients as gender neutral, there is clear evidence this is a mistake. Women communicate, relate, and learn differently than men. They want advisors who are coaches and collaborators, and they want to do more than beat the market: they want to "win" in the long run. Take a look at Figure 2.1 to review the key differences between the sexes.

Figure 2.1

Key Gender Differences

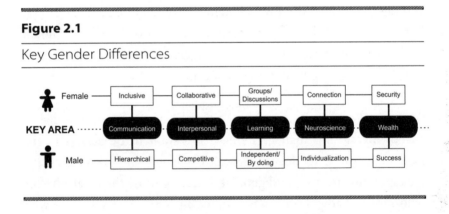

While you need to be careful not to stereotype an individual based on his or her sex, there are some truths about what it means to be a woman versus a man in our society. Most women want an advisor who has an integrated approach to wealth management, one who is both competent and caring. They want a professional who will take the time to know them individually, understand what it means to be an affluent woman in today's society, and appreciate the challenges and rewards of caring for themselves and their families.

If you take the time to understand and incorporate their needs into your practice, they will notice, advocate with their partners to hire you, and stay with you even when their partners are gone.

Your Next Step: Your Personal Definition of Wealth

Typically, women define wealth differently than men and tend to view money and assets as a source of security, not necessarily power and status. While there are exceptions to this rule, a majority of affluent women consider their wealth a means of taking care of their children, parents, and other family members. In working with these women, it is imperative that you know and understand their definition of wealth and also realize how your definition may differ.

Below is a coaching exercise to help you discover your personal definition of wealth. By tapping into your values related to money and wealth, you are more able to identify your strengths and potential blind spots when advising affluent female clients.

Set aside 10 to 15 minutes to do this exercise. It is best if you are in a quiet, comfortable setting with no interruptions.

Close your eyes and imagine you go to sleep one night to awaken the next day as a "wealthy person." In the time between going to bed and waking up a miracle has happened. You find yourself with more than enough resources to live your life as you wish until the day you die. Imagine for a moment what your first day living as this "wealthy person" would entail. What would you think? What would you do? What would you not do? Take the day one hour at a time, noticing each detail as your new life unfolds. Where do you work? Where do you not work? What activities do you engage in? What activities do you stop? Who is with you sharing this experience? Who or what would no longer be in your life? Just allow yourself to imagine the day in great detail. Once you have a clear image in your head, take a blank piece of paper and write about this experience. Use the above questions as a guide. Include any information you think is important or noteworthy from your visualization. You can write down the entire experience, jot down bullet points, or simply draw pictures and images to tell the story.

Once you are done writing about the experience, reread and review what you have written. Look for trends and themes in your work. When you are ready, write down your two- to three-sentence personalized definition of wealth below:

My Definition of Wealth is: _____

_____

_____

Now answer these questions:

1. How might my definition of wealth be helpful in working with affluent female clients?

2. How might my definition of wealth be a challenge in working with affluent female clients?

3. What did I learn from this exercise that will help me with my female clients? Male clients? Couple clients?

4. What action will I take today to incorporate what I learned from this exercise into how I approach and work with my female clients?

5. Who will I enlist to be my accountability partner for this exercise? This can be a coworker, trusted friend or colleague, or a spouse.

3

Your Affluent Female Client

> I have yet to hear a man ask for advice on how to
> combine marriage and a career.
>
> —Gloria Steinem, bestselling author and activist

THERE IS A MISCONCEPTION ABOUT THE LIVES OF AFFLUENT WOMEN. Society paints these women as either trophy wives sponging off their older wealth creator husbands or old matriarchs who spend their days decorating and redecorating lavish estates. I am not sure where these stereotypes originated, but they make me think of Lovey Howell from the 1960s television show *Gilligan's Island*. She was a socialite shipwrecked with her millionaire husband, Thurston Howell, III, along with Gilligan, The Skipper, and the fearless crew. While the others worked tirelessly to get off the island, Lovey seemed to spend her days mindlessly making wardrobe changes and flitting around while the others signaled for help. I never could figure out why she packed so many clothes for a three-hour tour.

The Lovey stereotype continues to be played out in the mass media. Classic television programs, such as *Dallas* and *Dynasty*, portrayed wealthy women lounging by the pool, looking beautiful, and waiting for their rich husbands to return home. *Dirty Sexy Money*, a short-lived evening drama, showed three generations of affluent women focused solely on finding love, shopping for new clothes, and worrying about having a bad hair day. Recently, celebrity reality television shows, such as *Keeping Up with the Kardashians* and *The Housewives of Beverly Hills*, keep the myth alive by not filming these women doing anything productive or meaningful in their lives.

All these shows have one thing in common. They all fail to reflect the complexity, talent, and diversity of the affluent female population. While there are still some "Loveys" out there, they are definitely in the minority. Real affluent women are more than one-dimensional. They are changing the workplace and altering the landscape of what it means to be a woman. These women are business owners, highly educated professionals, and philanthropists. They are breadwinners, wealth creators, and inheritors. They are mothers, sisters, daughters, and wives. Affluent women, like affluent men, are a diverse group of individuals looking for financial advisors who can help them navigate the land of wealth.

Affluent women, like most of your female clients, feel stressed out and pulled in many different directions. According to a 2005 Gallup Poll, three-fourths of these women are juggling multiple responsibilities, including full- or part-time work, caregiving for children and/or elderly parents, and engaging in philanthropic endeavors.[1] Their work and home life is similar to most American women, with the added burden of their being stewards of wealth.

Women of wealth each have a unique set of circumstances and prefer not to be lumped together into one broad client category called *affluent women*. Instead, they want advisors to ask questions to learn more about their unique advising needs. Like most affluent clients, they demand high-quality service that is convenient and encompasses all aspects of life. Surprisingly enough, they may be cost conscious despite their wealth. However, they are willing to invest in a competent financial advisor if he or she can help them save time and make managing, growing, and passing on their wealth easier.

> ### IN HER OWN WORDS
>
> *Don't assume that affluence means women understand how they got there. Many professional women, even those not afraid of numbers, still have problems understanding financial markets.*
> —SUSAN, 55-YEAR-OLD MARRIED FORMER CFO AND BUSINESS OWNER

GenSpring Family Offices invited 555 women with $1 million in net worth or greater to participate in a groundbreaking survey to find out more about their knowledge, behaviors, and attitudes toward wealth.[2] Based on responses from 115 women, here is what they discovered:

- Sixty-four percent of women surveyed make the majority of daily household financial decisions; however, 68 percent make joint decisions when it comes to wealth management.
- Seventy-one percent of these women openly discuss money matters with their family despite the fact that only 54 percent grew up with parents who did the same.
- Seventy percent of these women believed in raising children with a strong work ethic which included working for a living.
- Eighty-seven percent of these women felt strongly that those with wealth have a responsibility to give back to society.
- Sixty-eight percent of those surveyed reported searching for bargains despite their wealth.

As you can see, these women of wealth were not entitled spend-thrifts, but adult women wanting to raise financially responsible children, to be involved in their financial lives, and to be good stewards of wealth. Their desires were very similar to the men in their lives. According to Kirby Rosplock, PhD, the primary researcher on this study, "The goals of affluent men and women are for the most part aligned, it is just how they operationally look at their decisions and get to the end result that is very different." In other words, affluent women look through a female lens and make decisions about money, investments, gifting, and passing on wealth based on their family history, values, and personal worldview.

The Journey to Wealth

Affluent women acquire their wealth in the same ways as their male counterpart accumulate wealth; through inheritance, marriage, and/or professional accomplishments. In the book *Women of Wealth: Understanding Today's Affluent Female Investor*, coauthors Russ Alan Prince and Hannah Shaw Grove estimate that 40 percent of women attain their assets through marriage or inheritance. The remaining 60 percent accumulate their fortunes through their own efforts, including corporate employment, their own family business, and professional practice.[3] More women than men tend to be double inheritors, meaning they receive money both from deceased parents and a deceased husband. This may account for why the percentage of inheritors is slightly higher than what is usually reported for wealthy men.

A female client's journey to wealth is an important component of her money personality. It impacts her view of wealth, her risk tolerance, and how she prefers to interface with advisors.

IN HER OWN WORDS

Women are different from men and communicate differently. It matters how your potential client attained their wealth and what their personality is. I am very different from my mother, who was raised in a blue-collar home.

—KATE, 54-YEAR-OLD CORPORATE EXECUTIVE AND MOTHER OF TWO

James Grubman, PhD, and Dennis Jaffe, PhD, are pioneers in researching the difference between acquirers and inheritors of wealth.
In their article "Immigrants and Natives of Wealth: Understanding
Clients Based on Their Wealth Origins," they describe how clients
with the same amount of financial assets may think, act, and relate
very differently to wealth.[4] They use the phrases "immigrants to the
land of wealth" and "natives from the land of wealth" to describe the
diverse roads to affluence.

Clients who start off in a lower or middle economic class and accumulate wealth through hard work and their own efforts are called
"immigrants." These individuals have many of the same characteristics of people who come from a foreign country and have to acculturate to the new land of greater ease, comfort, and financial security. They may feel uncomfortable with affluence, struggle socially to
fit in, and feel alienated from their less affluent friends. Because they
did not come from the land of wealth, they may need more guidance on how to pass on family wealth and prepare their children to
receive the money. Often immigrants to wealth have a strong work
ethic based on their lower- or middle-class roots, tend to see financial risk as an opportunity to amass more wealth, and work more
collaboratively with financial advisors.

Natives from the land of wealth are individuals who were born
into family wealth and raised with privilege. These clients learned the
social customs and ways of affluence growing up and, therefore, are
more comfortable living in the land of wealth. Natives tend to struggle
more with finding an identity separate from their wealth and at times
experience their inheritance as a burden. Typically, natives are willing
to take on less risk than immigrants because they are more concerned
with wealth preservation than accumulation. When working with financial advisors, they tend to be more passive in the advisor-client
relationship and may be harder to actively engage in the process.

While the concept of natives versus immigrants is very helpful in
conceptualizing the experience of affluence, it is important not to

overgeneralize. There are exceptions to the rule. Therefore, the best way to use this research is as a guide to formulate questions. If your client's experience is different than this research suggests, remember that she is the only expert on her experience of wealth. Just like there is danger in stereotyping by gender, tread lightly when generalizing about affluent women.

Grubman and Jaffe do not delve into gender differences in their work, but they do touch upon the idea that wealth can be experienced as a burden for some clients. In my experience working with affluent women, I find many female inheritors who face a myriad of doubts when it comes to their wealth, ranging from feeling conflicted regarding their worthiness of receiving the money to feeling uncertain regarding their life path to engaging in self-destructive behaviors such as eating disorders, substance abuse, and shopping addictions. I call this phenomenon "the weight of wealth."

The Weight of Wealth

With wealth comes freedom and the ability to experience the great luxuries of life. However, affluence brings with it responsibility and questions that others with less financial resources don't have to face. For most of us, deciding to buy something is a function of our financial ability to make the purchase. However, if you are born into wealth or you acquired wealth through marriage or an inheritance, the question is different. It is no longer about financial resources; it is more a question of how do you want to use your wealth to express your personal values and create or continue your family legacy. Indeed, this is a more complex proposition than whether you have enough money.

In my work with affluent women, what follows are some of the common questions I hear pondered that contribute to the burden some women feel as a result of wealth:

- Do I deserve the wealth, and if so, how do I make the most of this gift?
- Should I tell my friends about my money or will that change our relationship?
- Does my romantic partner love me for who I am as a person or for my wealth and what it provides?
- What do I want to do with my life since my wealth makes anything possible?
- If I do choose a path, what if I fail and bring disgrace to my family name?

There are no easy answers to these questions. But as a female-friendly advisor, you can provide a place for your affluent female clients to discuss these issues. Give her a great gift by allowing her permission to explore her conflicted feelings about wealth and this, in itself, can lighten her burden.

Don't assume that because your clients appear to be comfortable with affluence that they are. Remember there is a stigma in our society against women of wealth, and these clients are often unsure with whom it is safe to discuss these concerns. Therefore, you may

---

IN HER OWN WORDS

I am often conflicted about who to tell that I come from wealth because I worry that they will judge me harshly for being a "trust fund baby." I did not grow up with flashy wealth, so it was always a family secret that we had more than others. While I enjoy the trips and experiences I have as a result of the money, I experience a great deal of anxiety over managing my inheritance responsibly and sometimes wish I grew up with less. People tell me how accomplished and put together I am. If they only knew how confused I feel on the inside.

—*MEREDITH, 32-YEAR-OLD CAREER PROFESSIONAL AND INHERITOR*

need to take the lead by wondering out loud with your female clients what it is like to live with wealth. Inquire as to the parts of affluence she enjoys and the parts that bring her angst. Give her permission to voice her negative feelings about the money and to normalize her experience of viewing wealth as both a blessing and a burden.

Not only can wealth feel like a burden, but for some it can be an obstacle to developing a clear sense of self and life purpose. It can become confusing to figure out what you want to do in the world when you come from affluence. Typical developmental tasks such as finding your first job, saving to buy something special, and making financial mistakes that cause you to go without are often removed. Being born into a family business may limit your exploration of possible careers because you are expected to work only for the family. Having access to a sizable trust fund may thwart your initiative to find out who you are and how you want to create a life of purpose and meaning.

If your client is lucky, she had parents who worked diligently to raise her with a strong work ethic and clear understanding of who she is in the world. However, some of your clients will not be so fortunate. In a presentation given by Dan Kindoln, author of *Too Much of a Good Thing: Raising Children of Character in an Indulgent Age*, he shared that many affluent parents fall into the trap of using their wealth to rescue their children from the normal growing pains of life.[5] While these parents are well-meaning, their efforts are misdirected and often result in the child not learning valuable lessons about self-sufficiency and problem solving. For instance, a father writes the check to the high-priced lawyer when his daughter gets caught with cocaine at school. No shame is brought to the family, the daughter avoids serving jail time, but the life lesson is lost. When you break the law, you pay the consequences. While no parent likes to see their child hurting, it is through these mistakes and the trial and error of adolescence that we become healthy, confident adults.

A note of caution: For some clients, the burden of wealth and confusion about their life purpose can fuel unhealthy coping strategies and

IN HER OWN WORDS

When I got out of college I felt lost. If I leverage my family money to help support an entrepreneurial idea, people will think my success is really due to my family's money not my hard work and talent. If I go into public service because I can "afford" to give back and still live a comfortable lifestyle, then I will have friends who are nonprofit executives who can't afford the trips and activities I am used to engaging in. If I get a job and make my own money, will my parents who gave me every opportunity growing up think this is enough? I envied the kids without a trust fund as my wealth felt like it made this next step in my life so complicated.

—PEGGY, *28-YEAR-OLD INHERITOR AND COLLEGE GRADUATE*

addictions. If your female client is overshopping, under- or overeating, or using excessive drugs and alcohol, then it may be time for you to make a referral. Notice the self-destructive behaviors you see in her, and express your concern for her well-being and your interest in helping her find professional treatment. While the tendency may be to stay silent around these issues, if you truly want to help her, you need to speak up. If appropriate, assure her that you will continue to work with her as a financial advisor, but her symptoms are telling you she needs professional help from a specialist in this area. (Refer to the Female-Friendly Resource Guide at the back of this book for a list of organizations that can help with a referral.) Even if she does not take you up on your offer to help right away, expressing your concern is important. It often takes several conversations before a client goes for treatment. Document any discussions with the client about your concerns, and note any referrals given. Also get support and consultation for yourself because advising someone with a serious mental health issue can be draining.

Sudden Wealth: A Blessing and a Curse?

Some women come into wealth suddenly as a result of selling a business or winning the lottery, or by collecting insurance proceeds from an accident or the death of a spouse. Depending on the circumstances, this experience can be very unsettling for your client and will require you to be skilled in the emotional side of money. Often referred to as "sudden wealth syndrome," symptoms may include, but are not limited to:

- Depression, sadness, and irritability
- High levels of stress and anxiety
- Isolation from family and friends who are not affluent
- Extreme fear of losing the money or rumination about finances
- Self-medicating by overspending, overeating, alcohol use, and so on

How well a female client handles receiving wealth precipitously is influenced by the nature of the triggering event, her financial literacy, and how emotionally prepared she feels to live an affluent lifestyle. Often clients with other psychological issues struggle even more with this transition. However, given the nature of sudden wealth, it is hard to predict who will have the hardest time with this adjustment.

If your client does display signs of sudden wealth syndrome, it is important to allow her to talk about her mixed feelings regarding the money and the downside of her unexpected financial windfall. When asked, most of these women would prefer their spouses or loved ones to be healthy and/or alive rather than having the money. Others long for the days prior to winning the lottery or selling the business since life and relationships were perceived to be simpler and more straightforward then.

With time and support from a caring and trusted advisor, most female clients eventually acculturate to the land of wealth. However, for some women the process may be more complicated, and a referral to a mental health professional or wealth psychology consultant specializing in this area is warranted.

A more detailed discussion of sudden wealth syndrome is not in the realm of this book. However, in Chapter 4, "Women in Transition," we will discuss tips and techniques for coaching and advising female clients during life passages, including death, divorce, and illness, that often coincide with the receipt of unexpected wealth.

Affluent Women and Work

More and more women are acquiring their own wealth through corporate employment, family businesses, or entrepreneurial pursuits. According to the Bureau of Labor Statistics, as reported in 2006, the percentage of women in the workforce had doubled from 32 percent to 62 percent in the last 50 years.[6] Not only are there more women in the workforce, but their earnings have increased. In the last decade, the number of females earning $100,000 or more quadrupled, with many of these women becoming the major breadwinners in the family.[7] No longer are affluent women at home, cooking and cleaning and deferring financial decisions to their husbands. They are spending their days in executive meetings, running businesses, and actively participating in financial decision making.

Part of the reason for the rise in power and affluence among women is that they are becoming more educated. In 2009, 57 percent of bachelor degrees, 60 percent of master degrees, and 52 percent of doctoral degrees were awarded to women.[8] This increase in education translates into more women being competitive with men in a variety of industries. While women's earnings still lag behind men's, the collective "she" is closing the gap.

Women are not only playing a bigger role in corporate America, they are also starting more businesses than ever before. According to the Center for Women's Business Research, between 2008 and 2009:[9]

- Women-owned firms have a $3 trillion economic impact annually and account for the creation or maintenance of 23 million jobs (16 percent of all jobs in the United States)
- 10.1 million firms are owned by women, employ more than 13 million people, and generate $1.9 trillion in sales
- 1 in 5 firms generating revenue of $1 million or more is owned by a woman
- Women-owned businesses are growing at twice the national rate of any other group

Many of these women business owners left the corporate world due to being unsatisfied with an environment where often women are penalized, overtly or covertly, for being female, for wanting to take time off to raise children, and for striving to have a more balanced life than their male colleagues. The flexibility that comes with being your own boss is very attractive because it allows mothers to be at home after school for the kids while remaining a major financial contributor to the family. For women who want to feel more in control of their personal lives, their careers, and their earning potential, entrepreneurship is a viable option.

This shift in women's wealth changes the landscape of what it means to be a female in our society. The traditional female and male roles are morphing, and individuals and couples are freer to decide

IN HER OWN WORDS

The corporate world is more about money, power, and status. The entrepreneurial world is more about stepping out of the box and being creative to solve problems. There is a freedom in running your own business that I did not feel when I worked for a large company. I feel I can be more feminine as an entrepreneur.

—KELLY, 37 YEARS OLD, MARRIED WITH TWO CHILDREN AND BUSINESS OWNER

who takes the lead at home versus work. As Betty Friedan, the 1962 bestselling author of *The Feminine Mystique*, wrote in the thirty-fifth anniversary edition of her groundbreaking book, "We may now begin to glimpse the new human possibilities when women and men are finally free to be themselves, know each other for who they really are, and define the terms and measures of success, failure, joy, triumph, power, and the common good, together."[10] This sharing of roles bubbles over into the advisor's office because no longer can you assume he is the provider and she is the caregiver. More often than not, couples are making joint decisions about everything, including finances.

A female client wants you to notice her contributions, to let go of the assumption that she is the less dominant member of the couple, and to offer services and products that cater to her professional as well as personal life. While she still may want you to create a financial plan for her family, she may also be interested in business consulting, venture capital opportunities, private banking services, charitable giving strategies, executive succession planning, and the creation and management of employees' benefit packages. Her increased wealth provides many more opportunities for you to serve her and become a member of her trusted financial team.

Workplace Challenges

Despite the advancement of women in the workplace, there are still some challenges to overcome, especially in the area of pay equality and leadership. Take a look at some of the statistics reported in The White House Project in 2009:[11]

- Nearly 50 years after the Equal Pay Act was passed, American women working full-time are paid just 77 cents to every man's dollar.
- Among Fortune 500 companies, women constitute only 3 percent of the CEOs, 6 percent of the top-paying positions, and

16 percent of the corporate officers.

◆ Among Fortune 500 companies, women account for 15 percent of the board members, and 13 percent of the companies have no women on their boards.

While women's wealth has increased, the lack of leadership opportunities and pay discrimination continue to negatively impact your female clients financially. With women living longer than men, these disparities are a real risk to your female clients' ability to accumulate wealth at the same rate as men and save adequately for retirement.

Hopefully, as women control more of the wealth and have a larger voice in the workplace, these issues will resolve. In fact, the same report cited above showed profits at Fortune 500 firms that most aggressively promoted women to be 34 percent higher than industry averages.[12] While it makes good business sense to welcome women into the executive suite, there is still work to be done. Until there is equality in both compensation and leadership opportunities for women, talking about and planning for this part of your female client's life is paramount.

Affluent Women and Family

Some affluent women decide not to work, but instead they dedicate their time to raising children and supporting their husband's career. In doing so, this does not mean that they abdicate all financial decision making to their partners. In many situations, these stay-at-home mothers are powerful influences in their husband's business and financial affairs. Many have had impressive careers of their own before marriage and children and are sacrificing their professional aspiration to do what they believe is in the best interest of the entire family.

Unfortunately, affluent women who don't have a job outside the around-the-clock job of being a mom are often discriminated against. I have heard them called "Trophy Wives," "Cupcake Ladies," and "Ladies of Leisure."All these names imply they have sold out and taken the easy road in life. However, motherhood is anything but easy. What in the 1950s was seen as commonplace currently is seen as radical in today's society—to be a full-time mother and wife.

The financial industry reinforces this stereotype by discounting the importance these affluent women play in family finances. The assumption is that she knows very little about money, does not care to discuss investments, and would rather be getting her nails done than attending a financial advising meeting. However, she is often the one to manage the family wealth while her spouse is busy running the family business. Just like any other female client, she makes the majority of the household buying decisions and is often the one deciding whether to work with you or not. Don't mistake her silence for agreement. She may just be biding her time until the car ride home when she can let her husband know what she really thinks of you.

Many of these affluent women are the chief operating officers of their families, which involves managing the family's real estate holdings, overseeing the children's educational plans, coordinating eldercare, supervising the household employees, and managing family logistics. In addition, many are actively involved with philanthropy and community activities, which require them to attend board meetings, fundraisers, and galas. While this may look glamorous from the outside, it involves a lot of hard work. By the time she hits your advising office, she may be happy to defer to her partner, not because she can't handle or understand investments and financial planning, but due to the fact that she is tired.

Affluent women are very influential behind the scenes, so don't fall into the trap of thinking your male clients are the only people to please if their wives choose to stay at home with the kids. The wife of a male client has a very important role in his success, and she is likely to be your client longer than he will be. So take the time to connect with her by finding out what interests her and how you can factor her advising needs into the meetings. Not only will this be good for her and please him, it provides some assurance that when her partner is no longer around, she will continue to work with you.

Affluent Women and Philanthropy

Affluent women give back to the community and the world. They are very influential in philanthropy and find great satisfaction using their wealth to improve the world around them, including others' lives. According to Melanie Hamburger, founder of Catalytic Women, an organization dedicated to women and philanthropy, "Women can be ambivalent about wealth and the power it brings, and philanthropy is an extremely positive forum for women and their families to engage productively around their financial resources. Good financial planning allows for some resources to be dedicated to philanthropy, which is where your female clients may get the most satisfaction in their work with you."

According to a study of philanthropic activities among high-net-worth clients conducted in 2011, 90 percent of women are either sole decision makers or joint decision makers when it comes to charitable giving.[13] The study also found that women practice more due diligence prior to giving than men, want to be personally involved and connected to the mission of the organization, and want to see the impact of their gift directly. A previous study conducted in 2006 discovered that 95 percent of women identified themselves as "philanthropic," not only with money but with time, knowledge, and expertise.[14]

Not only are more women involved in and identify with charitable giving, they give more than men and do so in a different way. According to a 2009 Barclay's Wealth study titled *Tomorrow's Philanthropist*, women in the United States give an average of 3.5 percent of their wealth to charity, while men give an average of 1.8 percent.[15]

Women tend to make decisions about philanthropy in a collaborative manner and consider their donation a long-term investment. Conversely, male clients often view a charitable gift as a short-term transactional event.

As a female-friendly advisor, you need to appreciate a woman's more collaborative and long-term outlook on gifting. While she is likely to benefit from the tax effect of her charitable activities, her primary motivations may be more about supporting a cause than taking advantage of a tax-free investment strategy. Therefore, ask her several questions about her interest in giving and how her philanthropy is connected to her personal values.

There are certain times in a woman's life when philanthropy may be at the top of her mind, including when coming into wealth, preparing children to receive wealth, and getting ready for retirement. Let's now take a brief look at each one.

Coming into Wealth

When a female client comes into additional wealth, either through the sale of a business, an inheritance, a divorce settlement, or a marriage, she often considers more aggressively pursuing her philanthropic interests. The additional money allows her to have a greater impact on the causes she believes in, and this sometimes results in her starting a family foundation. Therefore, when your client's wealth increases through one of these events, you may want to remind her of how you can assist in determining or fine-tuning her gifting strategy. Ask her questions about what makes giving important, what types of organizations or causes she would like to fund, and how you can be most helpful in the process. Because there are so many nonprofits in existence in the United States and the world, being a resource to narrow down the possibilities helps her save time. In addition, reviewing financial statements, structuring gifting vehicles, and assisting her in deciding how to attain the most impact per dollar is a valuable service for a busy, affluent woman.

A special note about widows and philanthropy: Often, recent widows represent a unique challenge to advisors as these women experience confusion when thinking about how historically they gave as a couple compared to how they want to donate currently as an individual. This is a natural and normal part of the transition process and is an area where you can greatly serve widows. Many women feel obligated to continue to fund their deceased partners' charities, yet long to invest this money in a cause that is more aligned with their individual interests. Others are not financially savvy and may be lured in by unscrupulous fund-raisers who target vulnerable widows for cash. By discussing how your female client made philanthropic decisions in the past and how she wants to make them now that she is single, you are providing a place for her to explore these feelings and become more educated about her options. This conversation often brings up guilt for the widow; therefore, make sure you validate her mixed feelings and normalize her experience as common after a loss.

Preparing the Next Generation

As female clients begin to prepare the next generation to receive and manage wealth, they often consider using philanthropy as a training

---

IN HER OWN WORDS

Over the past few years, I have been working diligently to figure out how to live with wealth without my husband to guide me. I feel extreme guilt over not wanting to give money to my late husband's alma mater. I would prefer to gift it to a cause that is more aligned with my interests but feel that my inheritance is still his money. I helped out in his firm in many ways and took care of the house and the family his entire career, but I never drew a salary so I feel like he still has the final say in my charitable giving.

—WENDY, 69-YEAR-OLD WIDOW AND INHERITOR

vehicle. Families will introduce children to giving at a young age and let them have input about gifting decisions. For example, a seven-year-old son may be encouraged to share his ideas about causes for the family to fund and then to perform age-appropriate research on a nonprofit organization as part of his due diligence process. Afterward, he presents his findings and recommendations to the entire family. Or an adolescent daughter may develop an interest in an antibullying campaign at school. To encourage her philanthropic interests, her family allots a certain amount of money for her to gift to the organization. As a learning tool, she tracks the impact of the gift on the organization and reports back to the family on a quarterly or annual basis. Both these examples show how children can learn valuable lessons about money, investing, and gifting by being an active participant in family philanthropy. If your affluent female clients have children and an interest in charitable giving, this is a great way to work with them to educate and prepare the next generation to receive wealth.

Retirement

Retirement is another key time for women to get involved more deeply with the causes they care about. This is distinctly different than how affluent men view philanthropy and retirement. A Merrill Lynch report found that less than half of men who were retiring planned on being more active in their community and more philanthropic compared to two-thirds of retiring women who had these plans and aspirations.[16] For those interested in philanthropy, it is a great way to remain intellectually engaged after your career has ended. Therefore, as part of your conversation with your female client about retirement, discuss philanthropy and how this may or may not fit into her vision of the next phase of life. Offer to help her evaluate this and to be a sounding board for these important decisions. Recommend she check out websites such as Catalytic Women, Women Moving Millions, and the Women Philanthropy Institute.

Remember, whether she is volunteering for a good cause, becoming a major donor of a nonprofit, or doing both, being a resource for her will strengthen your advisor-client relationship and possibly give you an opportunity to work with the next generation.

Now that you know more about the various types of affluent women, let's examine the top financial concerns that keep these women up at night.

What Keeps Her Up at Night

The biggest concerns of affluent women are the rising cost of healthcare, anxiety over not having adequate savings for retirement, and fear of raising entitled children. Let's take a brief look at each of these apprehensions.

Healthcare Costs

One of the top concerns for affluent women are healthcare costs. According to a Merrill Lynch Affluent Insights Quarterly Report, 40 percent of the affluent women worried about healthcare expenses, second only to concerns related to maintaining their families' standard of living.[17] Women make 60 percent of all visits to the doctor, spend two out of three healthcare dollars, and in wealthy homes make 48 percent of the household healthcare decisions.[18] It is no wonder why they are preoccupied with healthcare expenses.

There are no easy solutions since even Congress cannot come to a consensus about how to fix our healthcare system. Some women of wealth are choosing to hire concierge doctors to care for their families' healthcare concerns. While this helps ease their anxieties, it is a costly option and only accessible to some affluent women.

Your female clients need assistance in reviewing and selecting healthcare plans, planning for and managing the increasing expenses related to their health, and coming up with solutions to alleviate their fears. Being a resource for information on this topic and having referrals to concierge physicians in your area is important. Work to develop plans for mitigating this risk for them and their families. Validate them on how difficult this part of their financial life is, even if there are no good solutions, because having someone to discuss these concerns with is of great value.

Retirement Planning

According to a 2009 report, "The Impact of Retirement Risk on Women," women tend to be preoccupied with immediate life concerns and fail to look ahead at retirement. The survey found that 63 percent of women are anxious about retirement, compared to only 52 percent of men.[19] Although you may believe that women with adequate financial resources are free from this concern, they are not.

Affluent women realize they are likely to live longer than their male partners and understand that this could be a real financial concern. They often react to this information in one of two ways: they hyperfocus on retirement planning and possibly miss out on some of life's current pleasures or they put their head in the sand and decide they will worry about it later. Either coping strategy is not ideal. Your job is to help your female clients plan for the uncertain future by asking how they feel about retirement and what they envision for themselves, and by helping them take steps today to plan for tomorrow.

It is important to remember that women tend to be more emotional when it comes to retirement, and many female clients fear ending up destitute in their old age. Don't make the mistake of assuring a woman that she has enough assets to live on, yet neglect to explore the feelings she has about retirement. This will result in her feeling unheard. Instead, find out more about her underlying concerns by asking many open-ended questions. Coach her on ways this anxiety is helpful, that is, how it motivates her to save more for the future, and how it is unhelpful, for example, how it raises her blood pressure. Often she needs a neutral party to talk about these fears and to develop a plan for addressing them from both a financial and an emotional standpoint.

Raising Affluent Children

One of the top concerns of affluent parents is rearing financially responsible children. A Merrill Lynch Wealth Management report stated that nearly twice as many affluent investors said teaching their children "financial know-how" was a higher priority than teaching them about "choosing the right spouse/partner.[20] Clearly, wealthy parents are worried about raising children with affluence and preparing the next generation to receive and manage family wealth prudently. This is both an area of interest and a fear for your female clients. It also presents an important opportunity for you to strengthen your advisor-client relationship with them by coaching them on how to raise financially thoughtful children. How to develop skills in this area will be discussed in Chapter 9, "Preparing the Next Generation to Receive Wealth."

Summary

Affluent women live complicated, busy, and stressful lives. They are major economic players and will continue to be in the coming decades. These women are changing the landscape at work and at home. They are inheritors, wealth creators, and often both. They represent a challenge for traditional, transaction-oriented financial advisors and are now speaking up more than ever about their dissatisfaction with how the financial industry perceives them. While affluent women present a unique challenge to you as the advisor, they also represent a big opportunity as well.

As one advisor shared with me, "Affluent women need to unpack their suitcase slowly whereas men just show up, throw their suitcase in the corner and are off and running." In other words, affluent women have competing priorities in life, care for more than just themselves, and financially face many different challenges than men. A female-friendly advisor listens to her female client as she slowly uncovers the multidimensional layers of her life. The goal is to help her unpack her suitcase, plan for the various "trips" in her life, and provide her with the expertise she needs to enjoy the journey. And if you make a good traveling partner, she is likely to be a client for life.

Your Next Step: Study Affluent Women

Now that you understand more about the complexities and diversity of affluent women, you realize how much more there is to learn. Being a student of your current clients' female experiences in conjunction with making a commitment to learn more about affluent women in general will strengthen your ability to serve these women in your role as advisor. Below are five practical tips for studying affluent women in an ongoing way:

◆ **Read books about the female experience.** Books such as *The Feminine Mystique* by Betty Friedan and *In a Different Voice* by Carol Gilligan are classics that discuss the female experience and the challenges faced growing up as a woman in this culture. Consider reading one of these books, or a book listed in the Female-Friendly Resource Guide at the back of this book as a way of learning more about women's experiences in the world.

◆ **Observe cultural and media messages about affluent women.** Watch the news, network or cable television shows, and reality dramas, noting the messages that are sent to women on a daily basis. Ask yourself, "What messages are sent about women and wealth in this program or commercial?" and "Do these images match up with how I see the women in my life?" Discuss your observations with your female clients. Find out their impressions of how affluent women are portrayed in the media and its impact on them personally.

♦ **Set a Google Alert for affluent women.** A Google Alert is a feature offered by Google where you can automatically search for a particular topic and have the results of the search sent to you by e-mail on a daily or weekly basis. When selecting the words for your alert, consider the type of affluent women you work with or want to work with in your practice. Consider keywords such as "affluent women," "women and wealth," "women executives," "female entrepreneurs," and "women and philanthropy." Set multiple alerts to discover which ones yield the best data, and then delete the ones that are not as useful.

♦ **Sign up for newsletters and e-zines that focus on women's issues.** One of the best ways to get to know a client is to read what she is reading. Ask your current clients what websites, online newsletters, or e-zines they subscribe to, and then sign up too. Not only will you learn more about what is important to her, you will also discover more about the female experience in general.

♦ **Ask your current affluent female clients curious questions in every encounter.** The best way to find out more about your female clients' experiences is to ask directly. Each time you make a connection with an affluent woman, ask her a curious, open-ended question. This shows you care about her unique life experience and also makes being a student of affluent women a routine practice.

4

Women in Transition

One man can make a difference and
every man should try.

—Jacqueline Kennedy Onassis, former First Lady

IMAGINE YOU ARE IN YOUR OFFICE WHEN THE TELEPHONE RINGS. IT
is your longtime client Mr. Mayer, who is 62 years of age and worth
about $3 million. You have been working with him and his wife for
over 15 years. From time to time, you two get together and play
golf. He called today to invite you to play in an upcoming charity
tournament, when suddenly he shares he has been diagnosed with
terminal cancer. You are shocked. He seems so healthy and vibrant.
Mr. Mayer goes on to tell you his wife will be moving the family assets to her daughter's financial advisor. When you ask why, he says,
"She just does not feel a connection with you, like I do."

This scenario plays out in advisors' offices across the country almost on a daily basis. The mistake this advisor made, like so many
others, was to put all his energy and focus on the husband and very
little, if any, on the wife. There is a false assumption that if you cater
to the male wealth creator and connect well with him, his wife will
follow suit. This may have been true 50 years ago, but in today's

world this is a risky strategy. Or maybe you know you should take the wife out to lunch and build the relationship, but you just don't find time in your busy schedule to make it a priority. Either way, she is likely to leave you when the spouse is no longer in the picture. Every day that you put wives at the bottom of your to-do list, you run the risk of losing millions of dollars of assets from your business during times of their family transitions.

In the case of Mr. Mayer, the advisor could have invested four to six hours of his time to foster and build a connection with Mrs. Mayer. While there is no guarantee she would have kept her assets with the advisor when her husband got sick, there at least would have been an opportunity for the advisor and her to discuss it directly. Instead, the advisor failed to recognize and communicate the important role she plays in the management of the family wealth and will now spend the next six to nine months prospecting and trying to enlist another $3 million client.

If this case scenario sounds familiar, don't fret. The truth is 70 percent of women leave their financial advisors within one year of the death of a spouse, and the average age of a female widow is 56 years of age, meaning she has many more years ahead of her as a newly single person to be your client.[1] With only 30 percent of widows staying with the couple's advisor, it is clear that there is both a large problem in the industry when it comes to serving the needs of affluent female clients in transition and an opportunity for you as an advisor. Often it is times of crisis or family transition when a woman inquires about your services or becomes more involved in the money management. If you truly understand the psychological and financial aspects of women in transition, then you can use these times of transition as a way to solidify the relationship with an existing client or attract and connect with new ones.

In Her Own Words

My husband died suddenly at the age of 51, leaving me with two children, ages 8 and 16. He was the one who stayed at home with the kids, and I had "the fast track" career. All that changed when he passed and it took me three advisors before I found one that truly listened to me and did not make assumptions about me as a woman. It was a very scary time, and she helped me get through it a day at a time. I have been working with that advisor ever since because I really trust she has my best interests at heart.

—KATHLEEN, WIDOW, *50 YEARS OLD WITH TWO CHILDREN*

Life Passages

As human beings, we all go through developmental crossroads as part of growing and maturing. These begin when you are born and continue periodically throughout the course of your life, until ultimately you face and embrace death. Common turning points in life include getting married, starting a family, getting a divorce, caring for an elderly parent, retiring, and losing a spouse. These transitions are similar for men and women, with the exception of giving birth. However, what a woman wants from a financial advisor when she is facing a change is often different than what her male counterpart wants. Men want to know the facts and make rapid decisions. Women want to talk about their experience, feel emotionally validated, and receive coaching on options. Eventually she will use this information and these conversations to make the best decision she possibly can for her and her family.

The most common life transitions that bring female clients to your office include planned events, such as marriage, motherhood, and retirement, and unplanned ones, such as divorce, loss of a spouse or loved one, and the need to care for elderly parents. Each transition carries with it financial and emotional challenges and opportunities for the client as well as the advisor.

In his 2008 book, *Your Clients for Life*, Mitch Anthony points out, "Transitioning from one life stage to another can be incredibly emotional. When moving from one phase of our life to another, we experience upheaval and change. Our ability to leave the past stage behind and embrace a new stage is often a process of acceptance, rationalization, planning, and goal setting."[2]

From a psychological perspective, there is a reason life transitions are laden with emotions. It is our way of grieving as human beings, letting go of the past, and preparing and readying ourselves for the future. Even with positive passages, such as becoming a parent, women need to grieve what it had meant to be childless and all the freedom it entailed before truly accepting the difficult and often self-less act of raising a family. The transformational process in entering a new life stage is similar no matter what the event: reflection, mourning, and renewal. This human process is more widely accepted if the event is negative, like a death or divorce. However, it is important to know that positive life events, such as sending children off to college or becoming a grandparent, can stir up mixed emotions, too.

Experiencing, accepting, and when possible, planning for change is often best done in consort with a financial advisor. During times of transition, clients are typically not in their reflective minds, but in their reflexive or reactive brains and need help making rational decisions. A trusted and competent financial advisor can be the calm in the storm for a female client by offering a place for her to reflect, ponder, and examine various financial options related to her situation. But unlike many of her male counterparts, the female client also wants an advisor who can listen to her story and validate her thoughts and feelings. These emotions may range from confusion, embarrassment, fear, sadness, and anger to relief, joy, and hope. Remember that the female brain and how women are socialized in our culture allow them to have easier access to feeling states and a greater ability and need to verbalize them. When a female client enters your office after finding out her husband is leaving her and runs through a gamut of emotions, this does not necessarily mean she needs a referral to a mental health professional. It just signifies she has a female brain and is coping with the mixed emotions of getting a divorce.

A female-friendly advisor listens to her story and validates and normalizes her conflicting emotions. An advisor only needs to ask, "Tell me more about your situation," and then sit back and listen. While this sounds simple, for some advisors who are solution-focused this type of active listening is a challenge and counterintuitive. But it is an essential part of her learning and decision-making style. Reflect back the content of what she is saying and show empathy. For example, "It sounds like you are very angry that your husband left you. It must be hard." Or "You seem both relieved and frustrated that you inherited this money. I imagine that may be confusing." Don't be wed to being right, just to being curious. Check in with her frequently to make sure you have heard her correctly. Eventually, she will use these dialogues and data to gain clarity for herself. At the same time, you will be gathering important information to help you best serve your client now and in the future.

Rick Kahler, CFP, principal of Kahler Financial Group and coauthor of several books, including *Conscious Finance: Uncover Your Hidden Money Beliefs and Transform the Role of Money in Your Life* with Kathleen Fox, offers left-brained financial advisors hope. "My worst client used to be a divorced woman. I had very, very little chance of retaining her, and today I have a number of women that have lost husbands, either through divorce or death."

What changed in Kahler's advising style? He took the risk to just be with a client's feelings. "A client came in one day and she had just lost her husband, and I had all of my charts and everything ready to go to talk about her investments; and she said, you know, I was just diagnosed with cancer. She talked a little bit about that, and she started to cry, and I just reached over and gave her a Kleenex." What this situation exemplifies is that the meeting is about the client and sometimes it is prudent to put your advising agenda to the side. A client-centered advisor follows the lead of the client. "For me, it was an acknowledgment of, oh, there's a feeling loose in the room. And this is more important than getting into the mutual funds," Kahler explains.

It is not your fault you were trained to develop a meeting agenda and follow it. The dilemma is that this approach does not allow for a client's unexpected thoughts, feelings, and reactions to life events. When working with a woman in transition, it is imperative you allow time for what is important to her. It may be talking about how she feels or what she fears, or answering her questions. She may even want to see your charts and graphs. But the important thing is for you to let her decide and dictate the pace and content of the meeting.

As a financial advisor your job is to provide financial options and, sometimes, your opinion regarding how to navigate life transitions. But if you lead with numbers, don't be shocked if you find it hard to connect and collaborate with women. Women in transition want financial advisors who are willing to be in the muck of transition with them. And for many advisors, being in the unpredictable and messy world of feelings can be daunting. But if you rise to the challenge, your female clients will forever be grateful.

Client Transitions: The Advisor's Challenge

Why do so many financial advisors struggle with the "human side" of finance? Because, in the industry, the myth is that talking about and sitting with a client's feelings is not in the job description. In fact, if you are in a transaction-based, product-driven firm, you probably have been trained to skip over the feelings and get to the sale. However, in today's client-centered marketplace and especially when advising affluent women, you need to factor in the client's emotions about money in order to be profitable and perform at a consistently high level. Women want and demand financial advisors who are real and willing to get into the messy, emotional side of their lives. By allowing yourself not to know all the answers and to have feelings about clients and their life situations, you are proving that you are human, can be trusted, and will join with them when they need you the most—when they are not at their best.

You probably have been taught at school, at work, and in the financial industry mainstream culture that a good advisor does not show any chinks in the armor. Compassion is "too touchy-feely," and caring is seen as something that gets in the way of closing the sale. In fact, I have had top producers pull me aside at conferences and whisper that they are concerned and worried about a client. I often smile and tell an advisor it is okay to care about clients and then reassure him that his secret is safe with me. However, I truly believe when not caring about your clients is part of the corporate culture, it is a big problem. An affluent female client typically won't put up with it. And dare I say it doesn't work with male clients in the long run, either.

Ted McLyman, CEO of Apexx Behavioral Solutions Group and author of *Money Makes Me Crazy,* speaks to how ingrained it is to not put the relationship first in the financial industry culture. "Most people are trained to screen a client based on criteria that has nothing to do with a relationship: its first assets under management, then its occupation, then its zip code, then its country club. It's all very superficial things that tie down to how much money do you have, what is the time frame, and how much you are going to give me." In McLyman's firm, the advisors focus on behaviors and building a good working relationship: "We get completely off the (usual) discussion, ask why are you doing this, what is important to you, how is this going to impact your life, and how is this going to give you peace of mind. The product is irrelevant; it's the behavior that counts."

Another expert in the field of behavioral change, Dr. Federer puts it this way: "If you really want to be the one someone stays with, you have to get your hands a little dirty and get into the complicated part of people's lives and understand what money means to them and why they are doing the things they are doing." This cannot be done by staying in your head and checking all emotion at the door.

Meeting with a client who is upset, tearful, or scared is challenging for most professionals. Why? Because very few financial services professionals receive training on active and empathetic listening and behavioral change. The advisors who are good at listening to women often are the ones who are more intuitive by nature or grew up with a house full of women who taught them this skill. But good communication, listening, and empathy skills can be learned. This type of emotional intelligence training is offered in Part II of this book, "Essential Skills for Advising Affluent Women," because these capabilities are crucial. You may never be 100 percent comfortable sitting with a widow after the loss of her spouse or comforting a new divorcée, but it is part of your job. And if you want to connect and work with affluent women, sharpening these skills is a must.

You don't need to be a shrink to help your clients through these life passages. But you need to realize what each developmental turning point holds for your clients and how to be helpful at every stage in the process. Therefore, let's take a look in a little more detail at some of the major life transitions your female clients are likely to encounter.

First Comes Love, Then Comes Marriage

A new marriage often motivates clients to come through the door. A woman entering marriage for the first time is likely to be excited, nervous, and giddy about the pending nuptials. You can help ground her by talking about how her financial life is about to change and educating her about her options as a married woman. If she has substantial assets of her own, discuss the possibility of a prenuptial agreement and get her feelings about taking care of herself this way. Invite her fiancé into a meeting, and teach him about money personalities, values, and active listening when they talk to each other about finance.

If this is not her first marriage, she is likely to know some of the pros and cons of managing money as a couple. Discuss what she learned from her first marriage or any other long-term relationships that she would like to take with her into this union and what she would like to leave behind. Encourage her to think through the financial impact this marriage may have on any children from the previous marriage. Overall, provide a place for her to celebrate, plan, and anticipate this next phase of life.

For same-sex couples, the preparation for marriage or a civil union is more complicated financially and legally than it is with traditional male-female couples. Same-sex couples are allowed to legally marry in only seven states, including New York, Connecticut, Vermont, New Hampshire, Massachusetts, Iowa, and the District of Columbia. In California, Colorado, Delaware, Hawaii, Illinois, Maine, New Jersey, Nevada, Rhode Island, Washington, and Wisconsin, same-sex couples enjoy limited "marriagelike" rights available through legal civil unions. However, none of these same-sex marriages or civil unions is recognized by the federal government.[3]

For an advisor working with a lesbian client, it is important to be aware of and educate her about the complexities of the law and discuss ways to protect her and her partner's assets going forward. Unfortunately, there is still a strong bias toward same-sex couples, making it harder for gay women to seek out financial services. Be honest with yourself and examine your own biases. If necessary, make a good referral to an advisor who is comfortable and skilled in this area. However, consider challenging yourself to work more with same-sex couples because many of the emotional aspects of entering marriage and anticipating raising children together are the same as in heterosexual marriages.

Overall, marriage and civil unions are a great time to connect with individuals and couples. Clients are optimistic, often open to change, and want to create a life together that will go the distance. Educate your female clients and their partners to the fact that talking openly about money and resolving financial conflicts quickly is a key to a long-lasting marriage. This will help them invest the time and energy needed to do this important introspective and insightful work. For more detailed information on how to advise couples in general, refer to Chapter 8, "Advising Women in Couples."

Baby Makes Three

A chapter on women in transition would not be complete without mentioning motherhood. While not every woman chooses to become a mother, the majority do. The decision to raise children normally enriches a woman's life, but it also represents some psychological and financial challenges. When the children are young, many female clients defer the investment and management responsibilities to their partners. While this may be understandable, it is important for the advisor both to encourage these women to continue to participate and to clearly communicate that they are a very important part of the financial team.

To keep your female client engaged, you may need to hold meetings at the client's home or at times when the children are in school. In addition, tie the financial goals and performance results to how these factors impact the children and the future of the family, something that may be more relevant to her world. Discuss topics such as how to raise financially thoughtful children, family values relative to wealth, and how to successfully pass on wealth to the next generation. By keeping her involved in the meetings and decision making, you are communicating through your words and actions that her input matters. If the unexpected happens, such as a death or divorce, you are now in an excellent position to help her through the transition because you have an established relationship as a trusted advisor.

Retirement: Now What?

A woman's tendency to put herself last on the list often results in her not adequately preparing for retirement and thus underfunding her retirement account. Therefore, you have an important role in helping her set aside the time to plan for this important life transition. This involves both financial planning as well as life coaching.

Start by discovering what retirement looks like to her. The traditional image of retirement, that is, quitting your job and spending the rest of your life reading on a beach, may not be congruent with her wishes. Today, many women continue to work, full- or part-time, in their senior years. They also travel, participate in philanthropy, and pursue interests they did not have time for when they were busy climbing the corporate ladder and/or raising a family. Therefore, check in with your female client about her vision of retirement—if she is a member of a couple, ask how this image differs from her partner's, and work with her to make a plan for achieving her retirement dreams.

An easy way to help your client tap into her retirement vision is to ask her to describe what a day in the life of a perfect retirement would look like. Have her close her eyes and imagine herself living happily in retirement. Where would she live? Who would she spend time with? Who would she not spend time with? Would she work, volunteer, or do both? What role, if any, would philanthropy play in her life? How old would she ideally be when she transitions to this phase of her life? By taking her through a series of thought-provoking questions, you will help her define her vision, so together you can work out the financial aspects of the plan.

If she is a member of a couple, do the exercise with her partner, too; however, I recommend you have her do it first, without her partner present. Remember, a woman often focuses more on what her partner, her family member(s), or another person needs instead of her own desires. By giving a female client 15 minutes individually, you often get a better sense of her retirement goals and objectives.

Then invite her partner in, and do the exercise again. Work with the couple to help them discuss the similarities and differences between their ideas of an ideal retirement. Focus on the underlying values of each vision, noting areas of common ground. Often couples have slightly different perspectives on retirement, and your role is to help the couple identify each partner's individual values and thoughts and then to facilitate a conversation to help them incorporate these into a financial plan for this phase of life.

In Her Own Words

I don't picture fully retiring, but instead working less. I love what I do, so I imagine I would work a little, travel a lot, and do the activities such as cooking, hiking, knitting, and reading that I typically don't have time to do with my current schedule. And I would want to spend more time volunteering for boards and charitable organizations. I just can't do it all now. But then, I can.

—JENNIFER, 48 YEARS OLD, SINGLE BUSINESS EXECUTIVE

One of the key components of a successful retirement is finding meaning and connection on a daily basis. If a client does not find a way to redefine her life purpose during this part of her journey, she may end up living in isolation and being depressed. To avoid this fate, ask your client to think through what is important to her, how she would like to contribute to society as she matures, and what supports are necessary in order for her to thrive once she makes the transition.

If your client avoids talking about and planning for retirement, ask her what retirement looked like for her parents. She may have a preconceived notion of what retirement "should" be, based on her parents' choices. If she does not want the same fate, she may unconsciously avoid talking about retirement, and as you know, this can be to her financial detriment. Remind her that in the modern world, retirement can be an exciting and rewarding time in her life and is only limited by her imagination. Free her up to consider all the possibilities for this next phase of life. After she identifies her retirement dream, coach her on how to determine what financial resources she will need to make her dreams come true. With proper planning and support from you, she can enjoy planning and preparing for this next phase of life and even have fun with it.

Breaking Up Is Hard to Do

No one walks down the wedding aisle expecting to get a divorce. However, 50 percent of first marriages do end this way. The statistics get worse with remarriage as 60 percent of these unions inevitably end with each partner going his or her own way.[4] This means if you are in this business for any length of time, you will work with a couple who decide to divorce, be called upon by a soon-to-be divorced client to help her evaluate her financial options, and have many divorcées as clients. How you handle these situations determines if you are seen as the "financial advisor you have got to see" before, during, or after a divorce or the one clients know to avoid.

Take Alice, a 68-year-old housewife with a net worth of $2 million, who recently went through an unexpected divorce after 44 years of marriage. She was told by her real estate agent that Sandy Cove Advisors in Hingham, Massachusetts, would be a perfect fit for her because they specialize in women in transition. She did not know much about managing and investing money, but she did know she trusted the agent, so she called and made an appointment.

Alice told the advisors at Sandy Cove she was trying to start fresh in a new town and wanted to buy a condo in the community where she was currently renting. She had no idea what she could afford since all the finances had been handled by her husband over the past four and a half decades. What she needed from her financial advisor was help with basic budgeting so she could determine if she could afford to buy the condo. While this may have frustrated some advisors who were more interested in investing her $2 million instead of teaching her about cash flow, it was where she needed to start. "Baby steps are so important for women going through a transition. They can easily get overwhelmed, and our job is to help them manage their new financial responsibilities and listen to their thoughts and feelings regarding this new and often unwanted role in their life," explains Deirdre Prescott, founder of Sandy Cove Advisors.

Alice's situation is very typical of women divorced after decades of marriage. Her life has been turned upside down both emotionally and financially. She needs education, guidance, and a kind ear. Over time, Alice grew to trust the advising team at Sandy Cove and soon revealed an unsustainable overshopping habit that needed to be addressed. Through more financial education and coaching, Alice learned that her new financial situation would not allow for her to continue spending money in her current fashion for very long. After exploring several options, it was agreed upon that the firm would pay her primary bills and give her a stipend each month for her personal spending. In some ways, the firm took the role her husband had in the marriage. While this may not be appropriate or agreeable for all divorced clients, it worked for Alice. It also helped her see that Sandy Cove Advisors cared about her and would invest the time required to help her rebound from a very difficult life transition. She eventually transferred all her investments to the firm and often refers her friends who are going through similar life passages to Sandy Cove Advisors.

It is important to realize that when a female client is divorcing or has divorced, often she feels a sense of failure for not making the relationship work. As women pride themselves on being experts at relationships, it takes a toll on her self-esteem. Her ability to adjust and thrive after a split is based on her family upbringing and her beliefs about ending a marriage, the circumstances of the divorce, her level of emotional intelligence, and her financial literacy. As an advisor, spend a meeting or two just learning about this life event, how she is coping, and how you can help. One tip offered by Elisabeth Cullington, senior wealth advisor and cofounder of Wealth by Design for Women at HoyleCohen, is to initially ask questions that propel the conversation away from the balance sheet and investments aspects of financial planning and into the client's personal life. For instance, ask the question, "If we were sitting here three years from now what would have had to happen in your life for you to feel successful and happy financially, personally, and professionally?" This inquiry will highlight your client's strengths and assist her in embracing the opportunities involved in this difficult life transition. Use her answer as a blueprint for working together to put these pieces in place.

Remember some women may be very slow in this discovery phase and require patience. Your female client may do best if you initially give her small action steps and hold frequent meetings. The best model involves educating, coaching, accountability, and support, all aimed at building her financial confidence and skill set. Other women may be very financially competent and need less coaching and hand-holding. Often these women want time to share concerns and fears about facing the future alone and want an advisor to collaborate with while making important financial decisions.

IN HER OWN WORDS

When I became divorced three and a half years ago, I asked my mentors and most trusted advisors who they recommended as a financial advisor since my soon-to-be ex-husband had managed our money before our divorce. I then interviewed and reference-checked all of the recommendations and found that they were all patronizing, dismissive, and didn't really ask any questions as to the goals that I wanted to accomplish. It was hard at a time that was emotionally challenging already.

—STEPHANIE, 39-YEAR-OLD DIVORCED PROFESSIONAL, MOTHER OF THREE CHILDREN

Whatever your female client needs, make sure you allow time and space for these discussions, and don't rush to "fix" her problems. Typically, men fix and women listen. Remember the rules of the road for navigating the female culture. Listen, listen, and listen some more. She will let you know when she is ready to act.

There are many financial, legal, and technical aspects of divorce that are not in the realm of this book. Specialized training and accreditation is available. For instance, the Certified Divorce Financial Advisors (CDFA) designation was created to train professionals on the legal and financial intricacies inherent in divorce proceedings. If you are not interested in specialty training, you may want to consider, as a valuable service for your female clients, networking and/or affiliating with such a professional.

Till Death Do Us Part

If you are lucky enough to find yourself in the 50 percent of marriages that last, your consolation prize is your marital partnership will end in death. While most of us would prefer not to think about our mortality, it is part of a financial advisor's job to help clients plan for this inevitable life passage. Losing a spouse is one of the most stressful and emotionally traumatic events in a person's life. Whether it happens suddenly or slowly over time because of an illness such as Alzheimer's disease, it is often heart wrenching and riddled with financial consequences.

As you know, one of the goals of financial planning is to develop a strategy for dealing with end-of-life issues. It is better to address this element of planning at a time when your client is not in the midst of coping with a significant loss. However, sometimes this is not possible because the loss of a loved one is sudden. In this scenario, the client shows up in your office looking for financial advice at a time when she is least able to utilize it. Therefore, you need to be sensitive and knowledgeable about the grief process as well as competent in those financial issues that present themselves when a person dies. This is a tricky time for a financial advisor: you have an opportunity to shine and build a more trusting advisor-client relationship, yet you are at high risk for losing your client's assets to a competitor due to this life transition.

IN HER OWN WORDS

My current financial counselor has really missed out on deepening the relationship with me when I told him my mom died. A condolence card from him would have been nice. He hasn't called to ask me anything about my inheritance, and so I let my mom's financial advisor (to whom I had never spoken until after she died, but he was the one who cried when I called and told him my mom died) manage her investments, which are now in the estate account that he set up. It still is disappointing that my advisor has shown no interest.

—HELEN, *52 YEARS OLD, DIVORCED MOTHER OF A 13-YEAR-OLD*

The financial tasks connected with the loss of a spouse or loved one include settling the estate, paying taxes, dispersing the inheritance, and adjusting the surviving individual's financial plan to fit the new life circumstances. This transition time also involves recognizing and normalizing your client's experience of loss. The best ways to be there for your client is as a friendly guide who understands the nature of grief and as a support during this painful passage.

In her book *On Death and Dying*, Elisabeth Kübler-Ross, MD, outlines her five stages of grief and how a person typically mourns after the death of a loved one. The stages include denial, anger, bargaining, depression, and acceptance.[5]

Denial usually is more pronounced with an unexpected and sudden death, but it is part of all loss. It is a protective mechanism that allows a person to survive the initial shock and trauma of the loss. During this time, your client may feel numb and feel that the experience is surreal. This happens because her brain has not had enough time to process the intense feelings of loss and integrate this information into her psyche. Often a person is in this stage during the initial days after the death and maybe even at the funeral. The image of Jacqueline Kennedy Onassis at President John F. Kennedy's funeral comes to mind when I think of how denial helps one in the initial days of grief.

The next stage of grief is *anger*. This can be unsettling and unexpected for clients who have not previously grieved. It also can be a hard emotion for the advisor to deal with. The anger may be directed at the lost spouse, such as, "He is such a jerk for not going to the doctor sooner," or it can be misdirected at the advisor or some other bystander. When anger is misdirected, it is often confusing for the recipient. An example would be a female client being uncharacteristically short-tempered with you after the loss of her husband. You may resemble the husband, remind her of him in some other way, or simply be a person to yell at in the moment. Misdirected anger usually occurs when a client is not skilled at managing her anger effectively. The best technique is not to take it personally and simply validate her feelings. With empathy and understanding, the client's anger will eventually dissipate. While it may be hard not to get defensive, it really is not about you.

After a client passes through the anger stage, she is likely to start a process called *bargaining*. Bargaining is a psychological way of trying to feel more in control of the uncontrollable. You can tell a client is in the bargaining stage when she makes statements such as "If only I had taken him to the best oncologist" or "If I had only driven to work with him that morning, maybe he would not have gotten in the accident." You need to simply notice the client's desire to change the situation and gently remind her that she is not to blame for her partner's or family member's death.

In time, your client will discover she cannot go back in time and change the situation. It is then that she begins the next stage, *depression,* when she starts to feel the sadness associated with the loss and is often found to be weepy, melancholy, or depressed. These feelings may be intense, and it may be painful for you to talk about this with your client, but this process is a necessary part of grieving and letting go. The reason this can be so difficult for a financial advisor is because it is not associated with any action steps. Often the client just needs someone to listen to her and sit with her when she is blue. The action is simply to be with the client and remind her that sadness is an important yet painful part of saying goodbye to a loved one.

The last phase of grief is *acceptance.* By feeling and passing through the previous stages, the client accepts the loss and starts to move on with her life. She may still be sad and miss her spouse or loved one, but is now taking steps to move on with her life without this person. This is often a time when she can start to make some financial decisions and be more active in the advising relationship.

Figure 4.1

Advising Her During the Stages of Grief

STAGES	CLIENT BEHAVIOR	ADVISOR RESPONSE
Denial	Disbelief, Confused	"I know this is hard, how can I help?"
Anger	Irritable, Yelling	Do not personalize. Validate anger and frustration.
Bargaining	"If only x, then y"	Gently remind her the loss is not her fault.
Depression	Tearful, Sad, Irritable	Comfort and listen. Use deceased's name.
Acceptance	In action. More at ease	Coach her using small, doable action steps.

Source: Based on Elisabeth Kübler-Ross's "Five Stages of Grief" outlined in her book *On Death and Dying.*

It is important to know that the stages of grief are not linear. Clients circle back and forth through various stages. Clients who are not as psychologically minded may find comfort in learning about these stages, which should help to normalize their experience. You may want to ask a grieving spouse if she is familiar with the stages of grief. If not, ask her if she would like you to share what you know. If she declines, respect her decision and know that you have communicated that you care. If she agrees, educate her about the five stages. Ask her what stage she feels she is currently in and why. This allows her to talk about the loss and to see you as a resource for more than just financial information.

Avoid saying "I'm sorry" because this puts the widow in the position of having to comfort you. Also don't proclaim to "know" about her grief. Instead say something like "I can't even begin to understand what you must be going through right now." This statement validates her pain and leaves the door open for her to tell you more about her particular experience of grief. Also, remember to use her spouse's name. Many widows complain that their advisors and others stop addressing their husbands by their proper name. Again this is more about your discomfort with the loss than hers. So make an effort to call him "John," not "your late husband."

In Her Own Words

Widows are so vulnerable, and they're so concerned about being secure. Widows want to trust somebody. They want to believe that the financial salesperson is smarter than they are, knows more, and really cares about them. But they can be sold very inappropriate products if that person takes advantage of their situation.

—KATHLEEN, WIDOW AND AUTHOR OF MOVING FORWARD ON YOUR OWN

The biggest mistake advisors make in talking with a widow is to share a recent loss, making the assumption that her experience is the same or similar. While this is well-meaning and intended to help, it often alienates the widow. Instead, let her be the expert on herself by giving her the time and space to fill you in on her reaction to the loss. Show compassion and listen, which are very powerful ways to demonstrate that you care about more than just her money.

Kathleen M. Rehl, CFP, the author of *Moving Forward on Your Own: A Financial Guidebook for Widows*, offers these five tips for advisors working with widows:[6]

1. **Encourage her not to rush.** A woman who has recently lost a spouse often wants to make financial decisions quickly and to put this painful part of life behind her. As an advisor, help her slow down and carefully evaluate decisions that need to be made in the short term, that is, burial and funeral expenses, and encourage her to postpone other decisions that don't require immediate attention, such as liquidating assets. Often a 6- or 12-month "decision free zone" is a helpful strategy to suggest that will allow her time to grieve before making substantial financial decisions.

2. **Educate her about "financial wolves."** Unethical financial professionals often target recent widows because they are especially vulnerable and easy prey. Encourage your client to bring all offers to you to evaluate, and remind her that if it sounds too good to be true, it probably is.

3. **Assist her in making housing decisions carefully.** The house can be a reminder for a widow of her loss. She may want to change her living situation in an attempt to ease her pain. Help her analyze both emotionally and financially how a move would impact her now and in the future. While living with her son and his wife may sound comforting now, would she still

be happy with this arrangement in a year or two? Often the answer is no. Help the widow slow down and rationally evaluate home-selling decisions.

4. **Be a reality check for her.** This may be the first time she has handled the finances, so take the time to help her locate accounts, find out account numbers, and objectively look at her current cash flow and financial net worth. Small tasks, like filling out payment settlement paperwork on her behalf, can be a big help. Discuss and help her identify her financial goals based on her values. She may have different wishes and desires now that she is no longer married, so take the time to assist her in redefining her financial picture as a newly single woman.

5. **Make sure she doesn't become a "purse for others."** Unfortunately, needy relatives and suitors may contact her asking for money shortly after the death of a spouse. Encourage your client to carefully consider each request and to possibly put off all gifting for one year until she has time to grieve. There are men who pursue wealthy widows because the widows are lonely, in need of companionship, and have deep pockets. These men profess their undying love quickly and are out to make some quick cash or to find long-term financial security through unsuspecting widows. While this is not an easy topic to bring up with your client, it is important to bring it up if she starts dating soon after the death of her spouse or is writing large checks to friends and family members.

It can take up to one year to grieve the loss of a spouse or significant loved one. If you find your client is taking longer to go through the stages of grief or seems stuck in one of the phases, then she may be suffering from *complicated bereavement.* This is a psychological condition that is very treatable, but requires professional mental health support. While you can be helpful during this time, it is also important to make a referral when appropriate. Make sure you have one or two high-quality mental health professionals to refer your clients to if needed. Often in a matter of a few sessions, the client will be back on track and moving toward embracing the next part of her life.

Sandwiched In

More and more women find themselves caring for their children and their elderly parents at the same time. Referred to as the "Sandwich Generation," these women face unique challenges that were not prevalent for their mothers. Better healthcare, nutrition, and medical treatments allow us to live longer and start families later in life. Therefore, your female clients are often struggling simultaneously to balance their careers with their families and eldercare responsibilities. Not only does this put a financial strain on women, it causes these caregivers to feel more burned-out, overwhelmed, and "sandwiched in" than ever before. It is important for you to realize the emotional challenges characteristic of this life transition and respond in a way that is useful and productive.

Women who are caring for parents and younger children often battle with a host of conflicted feelings. A woman may be grieving the loss of her fully functioning parent while at the same time happy that she has the financial resources to help out. She may want to be at her daughter's hockey game, but feel compelled to be at her mother's doctor's appointment. She may want to take time for her and her partner to reconnect, but also want to catch up on the work piling up on her desk. Like the cartoon character Gumby, she feels pulled in many different directions.

Complicated financial and emotional questions abound for those caring for children and elderly parents. Should the family pay for professional services or have someone stay home as the primary caregiver? Can the aging parent still manage his or her own finances, and if not, who will take over? Do we pay for private school for our children or put that money toward the parents' increasing healthcare costs? Do the parents have a will and an estate plan that protect

> ### IN HER OWN WORDS
>
> *I never feel like I am giving 100 percent to any role I play. If I am at work, I feel like maybe I should be home. If I am at home, I feel like maybe I should be at work. It is a big adjustment to go from being a professional woman with no children to being a mother of two. I live in a state of constant movement and chaos.*
>
> —*TESS, 39 YEARS OLD, CAREER PROFESSIONAL AND MOTHER OF TWO*

family assets and communicate preferences for treatment and end-of-life wishes? These and other questions may lead to these clients feeling tired, overworked, and ambivalent.

Some female clients will not bring the topic of childcare and eldercare up unless you initiate a conversation. Help her talk about her feelings and beliefs about appropriate care for her children and, if applicable, her parents. Find out if she has a wealth transfer and estate plan to guide her own children with these difficult decisions in the future. If possible, encourage your client to invite her parent(s) into a meeting and facilitate a discussion about how best to handle this delicate situation. While this may seem like a daunting role to play, advisors who take this risk report these meetings as very valuable for the client, the parents, and the advisor.

A few years ago, I had an opportunity to participate as a family member in one of these meetings. My mother had recently been diagnosed with Alzheimer's disease, and my dad, her primary caregiver, was anxious about what would happen to her if he died suddenly. Like most clients, I dreaded the appointment and was nervous driving to the advisor's office. At first, it was awkward and uncomfortable. But within minutes of engaging in the discussion, the anxiety disappeared. For the first time in my life, I heard firsthand what was important to my father and why he had worked so hard to acquire wealth and financial security for his family. I experienced a connection and a bond with my sister in this meeting that I had not felt before. And I felt grateful and indebted to the advisor who facilitated the family meeting. While I only met the advisor once, I know when the unfortunate time comes and I need to settle my parents' estate, it will be comforting to return to him for guidance.

When advising a woman in the Sandwich Generation, it is vital to acknowledge and appreciate the stress in her life and make working with you as simple and convenient as possible. Help her think through decisions related to childcare and eldercare and normalize her ambivalence over how to spend her time and resources. By guiding her through this life transition, you are again demonstrating you are a trusted advisor who can be relied upon to counsel her and her family in good times and bad.

Summary

In this chapter you learned how to connect and effectively advise women during times of transition such as marriage, motherhood, retirement, divorce, widowhood, and caring for elderly parents. In the normal course of business, having female clients who request these services is expected. However, if you decide that women and transition is a niche you would like to pursue, there are certain concrete steps you can take to build your network, skills, and referral sources:

◆ **Consider CDFA and related certifications.** There are many business opportunities for financial services professionals and firms who offer highly specialized services in the area of divorce. Not only do these certification and training programs offer great training in the legal, technical, and emotional aspects of divorce, many offer referral programs for their graduates.

◆ **Network with divorce and elder-estate attorneys.** Divorce and elder-estate attorneys are great cross-referrals for you. Make a point of joining networking groups that are largely made up of these specialists, and follow up with professionals who share a similar philosophy with you. Some organizations to consider include your local chapter of the American Bar Association, the Association of Conflict Resolution, and the National Association of Estate Planners and Council.

◆ **Reach out to funeral directors and eldercare facilities.** While networking with funeral directors and eldercare facilities may force you to face your own mortality, these are great connections for advisors who want to specialize in advising women in transition. Often assisted-living facilities offer free conference rooms to professionals interested in hosting seminars for the residents and their adult children. Remember, if you host a seminar, focus on education and not sales.

◆ **Network with family and marriage counselors and other mental health professionals.** Many women enter therapy to help them cope with these life events. By connecting and getting to know counselors in your area that specialize in bereavement, couples therapy, divorce, and parenting issues, you will be able to help your clients with the financial aspects of these issues that are outside their realm of expertise.

◆ **Sponsor new-mom seminars.** Why not invite all your new moms or young moms to a client appreciation event? Make sure it is not held in the evening when it is difficult for women with young children to be away from home. Instead consider a midmorning breakfast or lunch with childcare included. Topics can include saving for a child's education, the financial impact of motherhood, and raising financially literate children.

Over the course of a woman's life there are many developmental changes and life transitions. Offering to help a female client through these planned and unplanned events builds your reputation as a trusted advisor and as one who cares about the financial health of women. While this requires time and energy, the return of investment is well worth it as your female client base will be grateful, loyal, and referral minded.

Your Next Step: A Closer Look at Women in Transition

Now that you know more about the intricacies of women in transition, it is time to ask the women in your life what they are looking for in a financial advisor during these stressful times. To complete this exercise, pick three affluent women to interview. The women you select can be current female clients, colleagues, or friends. To make the data collection most useful, select women who are not afraid to tell you like it is. Assure them that their opinions and ideas will be kept in confidence, and then use the chart below to structure the interview.

Example

	Interview 1	Interview 2	Interview 3
Age	62		
Marital Status	Divorced		
No. of Children	2 Adult		
Type of Transition	Retirement		
General Fears/ Concerns	Enough $$		
Financial Questions	How can I balance my daily financial needs with my travel expenses?		
Willingness to Consult	Yes, would not do this alone		
Recommendations	Offer online resources on this topic so I can read when I have time		

After you complete all the interviews, review the chart, noticing any trends or ideas you can incorporate into your work with women in transition. If you found this exercise helpful, expand your market research to include more women as a way of drilling down deeper to really understand this market.

PART II

Essential Skills for Advising Affluent Women

Building Trust

Trust is a skill; one that is an aspect of virtually all
human practices, cultures, and relationships.

—Robert C. Solomon, Philosopher

WHO DO YOU THINK IS REVERED AS THE MOST TRUSTWORTHY MAN IN American history? The *CBS Evening News* anchorman from 1962 to 1981, Walter Cronkite. He exemplified the essence of trustworthiness every night in our living rooms and even got tagged "The Most Trusted Man in America" before his death in 2009.

What made Cronkite trustworthy? He was intelligent, consistent, and caring. He delivered the news with confidence and heart. He did not talk down to his viewers, but instead talked with them each night. He came into our homes and reported in a way that made us believe in what he was saying. Whether it was the tragedies of war, the heart-wrenching assassination of President John F. Kennedy, or man landing on the moon, he validated the viewers' emotions. Cronkite's strength in character, matter-of-fact persona, and trustworthy voice reminded us each night that this country would celebrate together, would survive any crisis, and would prosper if we just hung in there together. Each time he signed off with his famous line, "And that's the way it is . . ." you knew that he would be back tomorrow to update you again.

This type of steadfast character, commitment to the truth, and leadership is exactly what affluent female clients want in a financial advisor. While it is no easy task to live up to the larger-than-life image of Walter Cronkite, there are some valuable lessons to be learned from his communication style and grace under pressure. His consistent transparency and humanness established his credibility and fostered an authentic connection with his audience. While you can't show up in your female client's living room every weeknight, you can interact with her in ways that demonstrate your strength of character, reliability, and honesty. By doing so, you will gain and maintain her trust.

In Her Own Words

It is more about the long-term relationship and trust than just closing a deal.

—JACKIE, *56* YEARS OLD, SINGLE, CAREER PROFESSIONAL

Establishing Trust

How can you establish trust with a female client? It is very similar to building rapport and creating trust with any client. It requires actively listening, putting her interests first and foremost, and being a real person, flaws and all. Women are wired for connection and want advisors who collaborate with them in a different way than most male clients require. A woman wants to trust you, but first she needs you to answer her questions, to not judge her for not knowing something, and to take the time to get to know her. Working with her involves more than just products, transactions, and trades. It is about cultivating a long-term, advisor-client relationship that puts her and her family's interests first and your profits and business growth second. Of course, she wants you to succeed, but not if it means using her assets to further your goals at her expense.

Women select financial services professionals similarly to how they hire nannies and babysitters. They spend a fair amount of time interviewing different professionals and trying to discern who can be trusted. It is crucial for you to demonstrate that you are capable, safe, and reliable, just like a woman's caregiver needs to be. Your client needs to know in her gut that you have her back. As part of this process, she asks numerous questions and does extensive reference checks. If you are used to signing on a new client in one or two meetings, adjust your expectations. It usually takes her longer. She is looking out not only for herself, but also for the future of those she loves. And when she finds the right match, your patience will be rewarded with her loyalty and word-of-mouth referrals.

IN HER OWN WORDS

My first financial advisor, Brian, with whom I still work today, is great. Even though I am a small account, he always takes my calls, spends as much time as I need to understand my investments, and factors in my whole life in our discussions. He is a wonderful teacher and is very transparent about his fees and what is happening with my money. I truly trust him and have referred many of my friends to him over the years.

—GRACE, 51-YEAR-OLD DIVORCED MOTHER OF TWO, BUSINESS OWNER

Creating trust with a client is not a onetime event. It is a journey that starts at the first meeting and continues throughout the life of the advisor-client relationship. The best way to establish trust with an affluent female client is to be **T**houghtful, **R**eliable, **U**nderstandable, **S**ensitive, and **T**ransparent. Let's look at each one of these traits.

Be Thoughtful

It is a tenet of good client service to be thoughtful and to make your clients feel special. While thoughtfulness is good practice in general, it is even more paramount when prospecting and advising female clients. Why? Because women pride themselves on relationships, and part of building and maintaining a healthy one is showing you care. Being considerate can land you the account, and the lack of it can be the sole reason she decides to work with your competition.

Thoughtfulness can be shown in a variety of ways, including asking curious questions, showing empathy, remembering small details, celebrating their accomplishments, and offering sympathy when life gets challenging. Thoughtfulness is demonstrated by treating your clients as people, not just prospects or assets under management.

Here is an example of how thoughtfulness or lack thereof impacted my own advisor-client relationship. In 2005, my mother was diagnosed with Alzheimer's disease. As you might suspect, I was upset and concerned. A few days after the diagnosis, I went to see my financial advisor for a regularly scheduled meeting. When I mentioned my mother's recent diagnosis, he nodded and then moved on to his preprinted meeting agenda. Over the course of the next year, he never mentioned my mom's illness to me, either to show empathy or to wonder about how it may be impacting my financial situation. This lack of concern was the last straw, and I eventually left his practice. His pattern of putting his agenda first and not being interested in the rest of my life left me feeling uneasy. Why should I trust my money to a guy who doesn't seem to care about anything besides his return on investment? And while this may seem extreme from the advisor's perspective, in my client's mind it made perfect sense.

It is important to display that you care in an authentic way. Women know when you are being attentive as part of a sales strategy and have radar for disingenuous displays of interest. Find out what types of client recognition and appreciation tools work best for you and stick with them. If sending birthday cards and handwritten notes is not really who you are, then pick up the phone and call her instead. Remember what is important is that you regularly demonstrate that you care about her as a person, not that you should do this in a certain, prescribed way.

IN HER OWN WORDS

My financial advisor always turns to me for expert advice on fitness at the end of each conversation. By tapping into my expertise, he is saying, "You are an expert in fitness and I am the expert in handling your money." It makes me feel valued, and I truly appreciate the effort.

—*MARIA, 48 YEARS OLD, MARRIED BUSINESS OWNER WITH THREE STEPCHILDREN*

Don't underestimate the power of being thoughtful. Check in with your female clients often. Ask about her family, her career, and her kids. Show her you care. It is not time consuming or costly and, when done well, solidifies the relationship for years to come.

Be Reliable

A main ingredient for building trust is reliability. The easiest way to demonstrate your reliability to a female client is to be consistent. Remember Walter Cronkite who showed up every night at 6 p.m. This is the type of steadiness she wants and demands in a trusted advisor. Prior to the economic meltdown in 2008 and the indictment of previously trusted investment professionals, clients were more forgiving of inconsistencies. However, in today's marketplace, showing up regularly, following through with promises, and demonstrating through your actions that you can be counted on is imperative. Be the professional interested and eager to assist her and her family every time you connect. Communicate online through your website and in e-mail, as well as during person-to-person meetings or meetings on the phone, that you and your firm are dependable allies in her financial life. Always deliver top-notch service and ask her often what else you can do to exceed her expectations.

I often hear complaints from my female colleagues that a financial advisor said he or she was going to check on a dividend payment or contribution, but failed to follow up. For some clients this is a simple oversight, but for many women this lack of follow-through is unacceptable. What you need to realize is that even if you have not completed the task, an update on the status of the item means a great deal to a woman. It shows you care, she is important to you as a client, and you are working on her behalf when she is not in your office. Do not leave it up to her to decide if you are following through or not; make sure she knows it with a quick e-mail, text, or call.

If you are a person who has trouble with follow-through or finds that you are so busy that items such as follow-up calls and e-mails fall through the cracks, then develop a support system for getting this part of your job done. Schedule a follow-up reminder in your calendar the moment you tell a client you will take action so you will get an electronic reminder in a few days. Assign follow-up communication to a junior advisor or your assistant, who can take this responsibility off your to-do list. Follow-through is the key to reliability, so make sure you have a method for proving to your female clients that you can be counted on consistently.

Be Understandable

Imagine taking a business trip to Tokyo, Japan. You are in your first business meeting in this beautiful country, and everyone is speaking Japanese. You don't understand the language. You look around the room and think, "These people seem friendly and nice, but I don't understand a word they are saying." You don't know if you can trust them or not since you are not clear on what is being communicated.

You wish you had a translator because you never had time in your busy schedule to learn Japanese, but you don't want to be rude and ask for one. You decide to smile and just pretend you know what is happening.

This same scenario plays out in your office daily with female clients who don't understand financial jargon. They want to trust you, but they don't have enough data to make a decision. Worse yet, many women perceive advisors who talk in acronyms as arrogant and insensitive; two things that won't help you land or maintain her account. So when you are meeting with a prospect or a client, make sure you use "client speak."

A colleague of mine, James Grubman, PhD, uses the analogy of talking as if you were appearing on the *Today Show* versus *CNBC*. He states, "Clients want information digested into clear, straightforward, understandable terms that address their real questions. They want someone who can distill the world of *CNBC* into the most compelling concepts and facts. This must not be done in a condescending manner; it must be simple, clear, and respectful." In other words, convey *CNBC*'s topics but use *Today Show* language.

The bottom line is you need to remember your audience. Meet the client where she lives and use her language as a means of creating and fostering trust.

IN HER OWN WORDS

I know you are an expert or I would not be here. What I need to know now is how you can help me, and I need you to speak in plain English to do it.

—MICHAELA, *32 YEARS OLD, SINGLE PROFESSIONAL*

Be Sensitive

The word *sensitive* can be tricky for some advisors to embrace. Sensitive conjures up images of men in touch with their feminine side, crying at the drop of a hat, and, frankly, weak. But in this context *sensitive* means being in-tune to your client's needs, thoughts, and feelings as a way for her to feel understood, appreciated, and cared for. Sensitivity, when it comes to advising an affluent female client, is a strength, not a weakness.

Here is a typical scenario where sensitivity is necessary. A woman walks into a financial planning meeting. She is upset because her husband announced he is having an affair and wants a divorce. She is devastated but trying to be responsible and look out for herself and her children financially. She has made an appointment with you to find out how you can help navigate this unplanned and unwanted life transition. What do you do? (1) Share with her the facts about how divorced women tend to live at a lower income level than married women; (2) tell her she needs to hire an aggressive lawyer to take her soon-to-be ex-husband for everything he is worth; or (3) ask her how she is coping with this news and how you can be helpful while listening to her feelings about ending the marriage? If you picked number 3, congratulations. You displayed a good dose of sensitivity. It is true that you may want to educate her about the financial perils women face when divorcing and/or advocate for her to win her fair share in court, but first you need to show her you care. By giving her time to share her story and validate her emotions, you are fostering trust and setting yourself apart from your competition.

Are you afraid that if you listen to her story, validate her feelings, and give her time to talk about what is going on in her life you will become her therapist? This is a common, but unfounded, fear expressed by many advisors I work with. As a former mental health counselor, I can assure you the role of therapist is much more complicated than simply listening and validating feelings. Furthermore, most helping professionals do not have the financial skills or comfort level with money discussions that you do. Therefore, your role is unique and much needed by a woman, whether she is going through a transition or not. Be courageous and allow yourself to be sensitive because she really needs an advisor who cares.

Be Transparent

What makes a big picture window transparent? You can see right through it and know exactly what is happening on the other side. You see the outside world in living color and can tell if it is raining, snowing, or sunny. You see the old man walking by and the young lady running into the building. Your view is unobstructed and clear. Nothing is hidden from sight.

Transparency as an advisor requires that you provide your clients with the same access and visibility they get from looking through a big picture window. It involves explaining to your clients in clear and understandable language how your office works and what you can and cannot do for them. Their confidence in your abilities and recommendations is fostered by your letting them in on your thought processes and your rationale for those recommendations. As Mark Delfino, managing director of HoyleCohen, a financial firm that launched Wealth by Design for Women last year, explains it, "Transparency is something where you let them hear and understand what you're doing in a logical way, so then they're confident because that makes sense to them." Transparency affords your client to truly know and trust what you are doing with their money on their behalf.

When it comes to working with women, transparency is very helpful in fighting their mistrust of advisors. Eleanor Blayney, CFP, author of *Women's Worth* and founder of Directions for Women, explains that women experience selecting and trusting a financial advisor in a way that is similar to the experience of hiring an auto mechanic. "I take my car there and I want him to fix it, but I have no way of evaluating his competence. I have to take that on faith. But, you know, how do I develop a relationship so that I feel confident about him?" Part of the answer is openness and honesty. In our case, that also means showing her what you do and taking the time to explain it in a way she can understand.

You may have been trained in your career to "fake it till you make it" and not show any weaknesses when meeting with clients. The traditional philosophy is you need to be the best and the brightest to win the sale. But if you use this approach with your female clients, you are bound to strike out more than you score. With female clients, it is far better for you to honestly say "I don't know the answer, but I will get back to you" than to try to fake your way through conversations. You will earn their respect for admitting what you do not know, and they will appreciate the effort you make to get them reliable answers.

Overall, affluent female clients want advisors who are **T**houghtful, **R**eliable, **U**nderstandable, **S**ensitive, and **T**ransparent. It is best to let go of proving your expertise and instead to work at authentically connecting with her person-to-person. It will be a refreshing change of pace from what she is used to.

Trust-Building Techniques

There are several practical strategies you can employ to build trust with female clients. These tips fall within four broad categories: office environment, body language, listening, and validation. Let's take a look at each one of these areas.

Office Environment

Don't underestimate the power of first impressions because they set the tone in your client's mind about who you are and what you stand for. These impressions may be accurate or off base, but regardless, they are real and something to seriously consider when working with women and wealth.

For starters, make sure your office is decorated to reflect you and your desired clientele. If your office is located in a sterile office building complete with dark mahogany furniture, you are sending the message that you are a man's man, a corporate guy, and all business. If you have a home office littered with pictures of your children with the family dog, you are communicating you are a relaxed family man. Each of these images is different. Neither one is correct. But each does send a powerful nonverbal message to your clients and prospects, so you need to be aware of them.

Female clients, sometimes more than male ones, notice and respond to office decor. Put the book down right now and look around your workspace. What do you suppose your ideal affluent female client would say about your space? Would she feel comfortable in your setting? Would she know you were interested in working with women? Would your office communicate that you are a good match

---

IN HER OWN WORDS

The advisor who I have is really wonderful with dealing with women. One thing he did that was very different was when I met him for the first time, he sat with me at a little conference table in his office. He didn't sit behind the desk, but instead, with me on one side. It wasn't like an interview. He sat with me at the conference table, and he had these cards that helped identify my values. We didn't actually get to the numbers probably until the end of the conversation. It was more about me as an individual and about my values and goals than it was about how much money do I have and how much money can he make for me. It felt more like a relationship than a transaction.

—KATHY, *47 YEARS OLD, DIVORCED, PSYCHOTHERAPIST*

for her and her family? Based on this brief assessment, what changes might you make to your office?

Consider adding a sitting area to your meeting space. While a big conference table is pretty standard furniture for an advisor's office, it sets up a feeling of distance and power differential that may not be useful when trying to connect with clients. By holding meetings in a more casual atmosphere than a conference room, you are creating a greater sense of community, openness, and collaboration, all of which are aspects most women desire.

Adding a few personal pictures, pillows, or a plant to your office also can make a big difference. If you feel you need more of an overhaul, consider hiring an interior designer who can redecorate to reflect your personality and make the workspace welcoming to your ideal clients as well.

Body Language

All you have to do is think about the era of silent movies to realize how much we can communicate using only our body language. Charlie Chaplin made us laugh, cry, and feel uncomfortable all without uttering a single word. Later when movies added sound, actors such as Dick Van Dyke, Chevy Chase, and Will Ferrell continued to prove that sometimes body language is more powerful than verbal communication. All any of these comedic actors have to do is step into the picture frame and audiences start laughing.

While you are not playing a role in a movie, you do need to be aware of your nonverbal communication during your client interactions. You want to make sure you are projecting confidence, trustworthiness, and warmth. Women are especially in tune to body language; therefore, check in with yourself from time to time to assess your nonverbal communication. It can be helpful to have a colleague observe you in a meeting and share his or her impressions of your body posture, gestures, and facial expressions. This type of feedback can be a bit scary to ask for, but it is very helpful in making you more conscious of this important aspect of communication. The overall goal is to make adjustments, when needed, so you can be a more female-friendly advisor.

Always maintain good eye contact and sit with an open body posture when meeting with a client. An open body posture is one where you sit with your arms down at your sides and your chest is in line with the person you are conversing with. As you listen to your client, occasionally lean toward her to demonstrate increased interest in the dialogue. Avoid sitting with your arms crossed because this is often interpreted as showing disinterest or as a sign that you have something to hide from the other party. Do not wink as most women find this condescending and offensive. Sit a reasonable distance away from her to show respect for her personal space and boundaries. Remember there are differences in body language between the sexes, so if you are a male advisor you may have to work a little harder to make sure you are appealing to her feminine side.

Listening

The biggest complaint women have with financial advisors is "They don't listen." To more accurately reflect the situation, I would change this statement to "They don't listen to me *the way I need them to listen*." You probably do listen, but you were trained to listen to find solutions and solve dilemmas, not to validate feelings. This traditional

---

IN HER OWN WORDS

LISTEN! Women are more relationship based and trust based than they are fact based. Without the building of trust and the sense that you "get them," women will rarely open up to fully reveal themselves, which is critical in understanding who they are and where they want to go financially or otherwise.

—ANONYMOUS, *WOMEN & WEALTH SURVEY PARTICIPANT*

listening method is very masculine and works well with the male brain. See a problem—fix it. When it comes to building trust with female clients, this problem-solving approach leaves women feeling unheard and frustrated. If you are married, you are probably shaking your head right now.

Part of this disconnect in communication happens because men and women build trust in relationships in different ways. Women get to know and treat each other by sharing stories. Conversely, men learn to trust each other by participating in an activity together. Men hit a few golf balls or shoot a few hoops on the basketball court and talk about the weather. Men can hang out for years and never talk about their feelings. Women can't be together for five minutes without connecting on a deep personal level. Knowing and factoring in this gender difference to your communication and listening style is an important key to establishing and fostering trust with your female clients.

A woman needs you to listen as she paints a picture of her life. She wants to describe every brush stroke to you in great detail and have you listen to her story. She wants you to be curious about her color choices, why she chose a certain canvas, and how it felt to create her works of art. If you truly listen to her and validate her feelings, she will begin to trust you. However, if you rush her, warning bells will sound that make her question any faith she has in you.

By knowing how a woman likes to share and be heard, you can make some small adjustments to your interpersonal style that will yield big results. Advisors who primarily work with women tend to schedule meetings for longer intervals of time to allow each client not to feel rushed in the appointment. They take time to get to know the whole person and really listen to her story. As Mark Delfino, managing director of HoyleCohen, explains, "It's not as prescriptive of a formula and process as I think many in our business would like it to be." His colleague Elisabeth Cullington, senior wealth advisor and cofounder of Wealth by Design for Women, goes on to say, "The client experience with us is one of genuine interest in being concerned for them and their well-being. And that is expressed by the type of questions that we ask, the length of time that we take, and our interest in them. And I think that that makes a big difference in building trust."

If you want to establish and maintain rapport with your female client, listen, listen, and listen some more. Not only does listening build a good working relationship, it gives you valuable data regarding her life circumstances, family values, and goals so you can craft a financial plan and investment strategy that truly fits her and her family's needs.

Validation

Helping people with money is emotional business, and working with women involves feelings. As mentioned in Chapter 2, "The Psychology of Women and Wealth," the female brain is structured in a way to allow women more access to feeling states and more verbal proficiency in expressing emotions. In addition to the hardwiring for feelings, women also are socialized to express fear, doubt, anxiety, joy, and excitement more freely than men. Put these two facts together and women want advisors who can tolerate and validate emotions.

Talking about feelings may be an easier task for female advisors because these advisors are working with the same brain chemistry and socialization. Male advisors must contend with a male brain and the societal message that men who openly express feelings are weak. While this may not be true for all men, it certainly is one area where men and women typically differ. The good news for men is that a little goes a long way in this area.

Here is how it is done. The next time you are meeting with a female client, whether she is by herself or as a member of a couple, notice what she is feeling. Pay less attention to the content of her conversation and more to the emotional component. Once you have an educated guess, wonder out loud with her about this feeling. Do not worry if you are right. Simply ask as a way to show you care and notice her feelings. Once she shares her feelings with you, state that you understand how she might feel this way given her circumstances. It is as simple as that.

Below are two scenarios that demonstrate how an advisor responds using a traditional approach versus a more female-friendly one.

Scenario 1

Wife: *My husband doesn't feel the same way and thinks I am silly. But I think we need to put more money away for the future. If not, we may not be able to fully fund our children's college funds.*

Traditional Advisor: *Don't worry. You and your husband have an adequate amount going to the children's educational funds and your long-term savings. Here, take a look at the numbers.*

Wife: *(Nods, then remains silent for the rest of the meeting. Remember nodding means she is listening, not that she agrees.)*

Scenario 2

Wife: *My husband doesn't feel the same way and thinks I am silly. But I think we need to put more money away for the future. If not, we may not be able to fully fund our children's college funds.*

Female-Friendly Advisor: *Beth, it sounds like you are anxious about the amount of money you and your husband have allocated for the children's college fund. Do I have that right?*

Wife: *Yes (sigh of relief). I worry about having enough money.*

Female-Friendly Advisor: *Your anxiety shows you care, but also, that feeling must be hard to live with. How can I help you continue to communicate you care while worrying less?*

Wife: *I never thought of my anxiety as showing I care. Maybe if my husband reminded me that I am showing my love for the kids when I worry, it would help. I do know telling me it is okay does not help. It is not about the numbers, it is about a feeling I get.*

Female-Friendly Advisor: *That makes sense to me. (Turning to Beth's husband): Do you think you could do that for your wife?*

Husband: *Yes.*

In Scenario 1, the wife emotionally shuts down after the advisor minimizes or skips over her feelings. While his intent may have been to reassure her, she experienced his response as dismissive. Worse yet, she might imagine that the advisor is siding with her husband. In the end, the advisor did not take the opportunity to build trust with his female client and may have inadvertently damaged it.

In Scenario 2, the wife is likely to stay engaged because she feels understood and validated. Notice how the advisor did not judge or minimize her feelings. Instead, he took an educated guess as to what the client was feeling, stated it as both a positive and a concern, and then gave her permission to agree or disagree with his impressions. He showed empathy and asked her how he could help. Notice that he did not assume what would be helpful and let her decide on the direction of the meeting. In the end, the wife felt connected to the advisor and got what she needed—reassurance. She experienced the advisor as helping her and also as assisting her husband so he could be more supportive of her concerns outside of the office.

The content discussed in both case scenarios is the same, but the process of the meeting is very different. By taking the time to talk directly about a female client's feelings in a client meeting, you are communicating that her viewpoint matters, her feelings about the financial plan are significant, and you care. This technique may go against your inclination to stick to the concrete facts and figures and leave the "soft stuff" to those other guys. Certainly, you can make a choice not to identify, label, and talk about your female clients' feelings. But if you do, don't be surprised if they do not stay with you for the long-term. Women want advisors who can validate their emotions, see these feelings as strengths, and collaborate on how to move forward together.

Summary

Women want advisors they can trust. You can show you are trustworthy by listening, being reliable, and being sensitive to their feelings as well as their financial needs. Take the time to get to know your female clients as individuals, and demonstrate in every interaction with them that you care about their well-being. Make sure you use easy-to-understand language in your meetings, and are transparent about your fees and investment recommendations. Remember that creating trust is not a onetime event but a journey that starts at the first meeting and continues throughout the life of the advisor-client relationship. By investing the time to develop and foster trust with your female clients, you not only set yourself apart from the competition but you show her and her partner that you deserve their trust now and for many years to come.

Your Next Step: Who Do You Trust?

Take a blank piece of paper and split it into three columns. At the top of each column, write the name of a person in your life, past or present, whom you trust implicitly. Under each name, write down three to five traits this person possesses that instills trust in you. Also write down three to five specific actions or behaviors this person engages in that fosters your faith. Once you finish all three columns, review the data to identify trends and commonalities. Are the traits listed ones that you possess? If so, how do you show these more transparently to your clients? If not, how can you build these characteristics into your advising style? Are those actions that foster your trust ones that you engage in with clients? If so, how can you do more of this type of action? If not, how can you start to adopt some of these behaviors so they become habits?

Example

	Brian	**William**	**Wendy**
Traits:	Nurturing Loyal Supportive Honest	Consistent Loyal Honest Has integrity	Nurturing Loyal Open-minded Accepting
Actions:	Talks with me Collaborates/Plans Validates feelings	Responsible with $$ E-mails regularly Reassures me	Talks with me E-mails regularly Validates feelings

Trends Identified

Traits:	Loyal and honest
Actions:	Talks, e-mails, and validates

6

Active Listening

Courage is what it takes to stand up and speak.
Courage is also what it takes to sit down and listen.

—Sir Winston Churchill, former British Prime Minister

REMEMBER THE VAUDEVILLE BASEBALL COMEDY SKETCH PERFORMED by Abbott and Costello called "Who's on First"? It begins with Abbott telling Costello that "who's on first, what's on second, and I don't know is on third." Costello becomes frustrated as he believes Abbott is answering his question with another question. He does not realize that the first baseman's name is actually "Who." This routine became famous and is funny because the story line resonates with most of us. All of us have had the experience of communicating with another person and feeling like you are talking in circles. If you are lucky, the conversation ends with both of you laughing at the absurdity of it all.

When miscommunication happens between a client and an advisor, it is no laughing matter. Female clients want advisors who are effective communicators and will fire those who are not skilled in this area. The female majority demands that you communicate clearly, ask thought-provoking questions, and listen carefully. Women want to tell their story and be heard, and if you are not able to provide this type of environment, they will leave. The most frequent complaint made by the women I interviewed for this book was that financial professionals don't listen. When an advisor did actively listen, the client not only hired the professional to manage her money, but referred friends, family members, and acquaintances as well. Being listened to makes women feel special. It provides an opportunity in their busy lives to slow down and identify and define their visions and how they can use their wealth to reach these goals. In a world where women are being bombarded by demands and information constantly, spending an hour or two listening to one of them is a gift. Listening engenders trust and confidence in you as their advisor.

Advisors who are effective communicators are viewed more favorably by all female clients and instill a greater level of trust than those who are not skilled in this area. One study found that advisors who were perceived as good listeners had clients who were three times more loyal and four times more likely to refer friends and family.[1] In general, learning how to listen and communicate is good for your clients and great for your business.

Listening is a key component for effective communication; however, there are other skills involved as well. Before we delve into active listening skills, let's take a brief look at the other components of good communication. These include interviewing skills, managing

---

IN HER OWN WORDS

My advice is to be a better communicator—listen more, be sure that the person you are speaking with understands your financial jargon, but don't be condescending. Even though she may not understand finances like you do, she may be a very smart, savvy person and wants to be treated that way.

—BETTY, *60 YEARS OLD, MARRIED WITH FOUR CHILDREN AND A BUSINESS OWNER*

the process, using nontechnical language, and practicing good advisor self-management.

Interviewing Skills

Good interviewing involves asking thought-provoking questions to solicit information about your client. Financial services professionals who demonstrate excellent interviewing skills are curious about quantitative data, but also about qualitative data, such as money personalities, family values, and life dreams related to the preservation, accumulation, and transfer of wealth. They do not accept a client's answers at face value, but take an extra step and dig a little further to see if there is more to uncover and understand.

Good interviewing does not involve asking a series of scripted questions in order to sell a product or a service. Some sales training programs teach you a cookie-cutter approach to interviewing. You ask "x" and if the client says "y," you sell them "z." This sales approach turns female clients off and is one of the quickest ways to lose her account. The reason? It is advisor-centric, not client-centric. In other words, it often focuses on filling the advisor's wallet at the expense of or with little consideration for meeting the female clients' needs. Sound interviewing technique is always about the clients, not the advisor. It is aimed at more deeply understanding their world so you can better fulfill your fiduciary responsibility.

Asking good questions is an important component of interviewing. There are two types of questions: closed ended and open ended. Closed-ended questions are inquiries that require a "yes," "no," or one-word answer. These questions usually start with words such as "Can," "Do," and "Who" and are used to gather factual information. Examples of closed-ended questions include "Do you put money in a retirement fund?" "Can you tolerate risk?" or "Who manages the investment account?" These inquiries result in one-word answers, are fairly superficial, and do not move the conversation forward.

Therefore, closed-ended questions should be used sparingly in client interviews.

Open-ended questions are thought-provoking inquiries and require more than one-word answers. These questions encourage clients to ponder and provide additional data about their worldview and values. Open-ended questions move the dialogue forward and usually start with words such as "How," "Why," or "What." Examples include "How did you decide to start a charitable foundation?" "Why did you invest in this fund?" and "What contributed to your decision to start a business of your own?" The most powerful and impactful questions start with the word "What" and encourage the client to share how she made a decision and what values were a part of her thought process. While open-ended questions can also start with "Why," these inquiries tend to result in a client telling a story instead of her providing insight into her world. For instance, you could ask "Why are you here today?" or "What brought you in today?" These are basically the same questions, but with a subtle difference. The "What" question gets to the heart of the matter quickly and is more likely to produce useful information about her motives and needs for this appointment. Therefore, work at asking more "What" questions in your meetings.

When interviewing a client, it is also important to use clarifying questions. These are open-ended questions used to drill down into your client's answers so you know explicitly what is being communicated. Here's an example. If a client shares she is concerned about her children from her first marriage not inheriting the same wealth as her stepchildren, ask her this clarifying question, "What is contributing to this concern?" The answer assists you in understanding your client's motives and helps you gather more data. The nice part about clarifying questions is they not only help you gain clarity but also help your client gain clarity. This process of uncovering the answers together strengthens your relationship with the client and fosters trust.

IN HER OWN WORDS

Do not pigeonhole women. You are working with individuals, you need to understand where the individual is coming from, their fears, goals, and what they are comfortable with.

—CONNIE, *59 YEARS OLD, MARRIED MOTHER OF FOUR, GRANDMOTHER OF SIX,*

AND BUSINESSWOMAN

A simple tool to improve your interviewing technique is to look at each client meeting as an experiment. As an advisor, you are a scientist; your client is your subject. The discussion in the client meeting is your way of testing out a hypothesis about what your client needs now and in the future. To test your hypothesis, ask a series of open-ended questions and with each inquiry drill deeper into the topic area using clarifying questions. Eventually you will have ample data to support or disapprove your original educated guess and be in a better position to serve the client and her family. Here is how this tool works:

Hypothesis: Client seems concerned about her 16-year-old daughter spending too much money. Some coaching on raising a financially responsible child may be helpful.

Advisor: *You seem concerned about your 16-year-old and her spending. Is it okay with you if we spend a few minutes on that topic in today's meeting?*

Client: *Yes, Michelle's spending is troubling, and I am extremely frustrated.*

Advisor: *What specific behaviors trouble and frustrate you?*

Client: *Michelle has gone over her debt card limit the past three months. Each time that I tell her this is unacceptable, she agrees to spend less and then does the same thing.*

Advisor: *That sounds frustrating. Other than talking to her about her spending habits, what else have you tried?*

Client: *I am tempted to cut up her debt card and stop funding the account. I realize this is extreme, but I am so angry that she does not appreciate how hard I work to support her and her brother.*

Advisor: *What else have you considered?*

Client: *I have thought of bringing her to the office and having her work in the mailroom at minimum wage as a way to reimburse me for the bank fees charged for the overdrafts as well as the extra money she spent over and above her allowance. What do you think?*

Advisor: *Interesting concept. It would teach her about the connection between making money and spending money, which sounds important to you.*

Client: *I like it. It makes me feel like I am doing something to teach her about money and my value about working hard.*

Advisor: *Why don't you try it for a month and then let me know how it is going?*

Client: *Sounds good. Thank you.*

The above example illustrates good interviewing skills and the use of open-ended and clarifying questions. Not only did the advisor uncover the source of the client's frustration, but he validated her feelings. Lastly, he did not rush to provide solutions, but rather helped her brainstorm solutions that tied in with her personal value system. By spending a few minutes discussing this "softer" financial concern, the client feels relieved and grateful. Overall, this advisor's curiosity helped him facilitate a very useful dialogue that provided the client with insight and a plan to address her parenting dilemma. It showed the client that the advisor cared about her feelings and is a resource for more than just investments.

Remember, women tend to learn through discussion and bond through sharing details of their lives. Therefore, interviewing and having a dialogue like the one mentioned above is a great way to connect with, educate, and retain female clients.

Managing the Interviewing Process

All communication involves (1) content, the words used in the meeting, and (2) process, the dynamic and the flow of the conversation between you and the client. You may have a tendency to pay attention only to the content, but there is great value in also attending to the process of the interview. Managing the process is one tool that is simple to implement in your meetings. It builds trust, provides safety, and allows your client to control the direction of the discussion.

Managing the process involves checking in with your client to ask permission about the direction you think the meeting should take. When asked, she can agree, disagree, or make a counteroffer. This affords the client control over the meeting agenda and what she shares with you. As an advisor, it is important not to be attached to your client's answer. Trust she will know what is in her best interest and how to manage her time.

An example of managing the process is depicted below:

Client: *Hi Joe. Sorry I am late. (She is clearly frustrated.)*

Advisor: *You seem upset.*

Client: *Yes, sometimes working with your family is a pain. Sorry. We can move on.*

Advisor: *We can move to your portfolio review, but I am wondering if it would be helpful for you to talk about what is going on before we review your investments?*

Client: *I guess I should talk to someone about it. Lord knows I can't talk to my father about my concerns.*

Your female client works in a family business and has had a disagreement with her father, the patriarch of the family business, just before your meeting. They argued over succession planning, and your client is frustrated her father won't seriously sit down with her and discuss this topic. It would be useful to your client to have a dialogue about her concerns regarding the lack of a formal succession plan in the family business and her desire to make arrangements for the time when her father is no longer able to act as president and CEO. By being curious and open to talking about what is going on in her life before the investment review, you discover important information about her vision for the company and the family issues she is currently faced with. You may have missed out on this vital data had you not taken the time to notice her feelings and ask her permission to discuss them.

When using this communication tool, it is important to remember that the client sets the agenda and the advisor follows her lead. Letting the client set the pace, content, and tone of the meeting can make you feel a little out of control at first. But in time you will discover how valuable this technique is to building trust and safety between you and the client. It takes the pressure off of you to dictate the meeting agenda, and it is stunning how when left to her own devices, the client really does know what she needs.

Speaking in Plain English

In Chapter 5, "Building Trust," the importance of using understandable language with female clients by minimizing or eliminating financial jargon from your client conversations was discussed. Speaking in plain English helps your client understand her choices so she can make educated decisions about her future. It also helps you two connect and collaborate in a way that feels real and authentic to her.

It can be hard to stop using jargon, especially as your financial expertise and experience grows over time. Jennifer Moran, CFP, client advisor at Daintree Advisors, shared that when she started out working as an advisor it was easier to speak in clear and understandable language in client meetings. However, as her expertise grew, she would catch herself using jargon more often. To combat this tendency, she recommends advisors work in teams whenever possible. This allows one advisor to make the presentation and the other to observe and be on jargon patrol. If the observer notices the client demonstrating body language and facial expressions that indicate confusion, he or she can politely interrupt the presenter and ask for clarification of technical concepts. This allows the client to save face, but also is a reminder to the advisor to adjust his or her language.

If it is not practical for you to work with a partner, then you can try another strategy aimed at reducing the use of jargon. Ask a few clients if you can audio-record meetings. Explain that the purpose of the tape is to improve your communication skills and that it will be kept in confidence and promptly destroyed after it is reviewed. Later, listen to the tapes and note how many times you used technical language where you could have inserted "client-speak." Consider alternative ways of communicating the information so that the next time you are in a similar situation, you have an idea of how to talk about the concept or the recommendation using nontechnical, client-friendly language.

Another way to make sure you are communicating clearly is to empower your clients to stop you when you use words or concepts

In Her Own Words

I've been in meetings with my husband and I am just not getting it, and the advisor we are working with doesn't seem to notice. He and his colleagues use acronyms that I don't understand and show charts made up of walls of numbers.

—*KAREN, 33 YEARS OLD, MARRIED STAY-AT-HOME MOTHER OF TWO*

they are unfamiliar with. Remember, many female clients have been socialized to listen politely and not interrupt even if they don't understand what is being said. You need to give them permission to interrupt; but once you do, it will go a long way toward developing a healthy working relationship and showing her that you want what is best for her.

Advisor Self-Management

The last communication skill is self-management. This refers to knowing your biases and triggers and learning how to manage these thoughts and feelings in meetings. An advisor who practices good self-management only provides personal opinions when asked by the client or when he feels that expressing these insights are in the best interest of a client. At times, it can be complicated to tease out what you are sharing to further your own agenda versus the client's. This is especially true when a client triggers a strong emotional reaction in you. For example, it may be difficult to advise a new widow right after your dad passes away because she reminds you of your mother and this situation hits too close to home. In this instance, you may refer the client out to a colleague until your personal situation and wounds have had time to heal. However, it may be less situational as in the case of a client who incenses you because she never follows your recommendations. While you may want to yell at her, you need to remain calm and figure out ways to coach her toward action.

A large part of advisor self-management involves being aware of your trigger points and limitations. Consulting with a trusted colleague or executive coach can help you sort through the best course of action. Ironically, being a good communicator involves knowing when not to say something just as much as it does learning how to share.

Active Listening

The cornerstone of good communication is active listening. Active listening, unlike passive listening, involves attending to the speaker in a way that validates her feelings and moves the conversation forward toward mutual understanding. When you are active listening, you are not worried about what you are about to say next or what you can offer to counter the speaker's point. You are only paying attention to her verbal and nonverbal communication so that you can reflect back what you heard to ensure you comprehended the essence of the message. Your sole purpose is to be present for the client, to hear what she is saying, and to mirror back what she has communicated to you.

The belief that you have to prove your expertise quickly often gets in the way of listening to a client. Time and time again, I hear complaints from female clients about how an advisor boasted about his accomplishments during the first meeting, but failed to ask her any pertinent questions. Take the pressure off yourself and sit back and get to know her. Trust me, she knows you are competent. What she really wants to know is, do you care

---

In Her Own Words

Spend time discovering her story, rather than telling yours.
—*Eleanor Blayney, CFP, author of Women's Worth*

The following is a formula for active listening. When first learning this communication skill, it helps to have some simple and practical steps to follow. Eventually, when you master the art of active listening, these steps will become second nature.

Step 1: The advisor asks an open-ended question to start the dialogue.

These questions, called door-openers, are general and allow the client to open up about a particular topic.

Advisor: *What is going on in your business?*

Client: *We have hired a few new people and sales are up, but I have not been sleeping much recently.*

Notice this question requires more than a one-word answer. It allows the client to talk more about a particular area that impacts her financial life. The way the question is framed allows the client to share information relative to the business that she feels is important and that which is on the top of her mind. In this instance, the client shared data that was more emotionally based than financially. The advisor took her lead.

Step 2: The advisor asks a clarifying question to learn more about the client's situation.

Advisor: *I am sorry to hear you are not sleeping well. What is keeping you up at night?*

Client: *I worry a lot about keeping my business viable so I can meet payroll and take care of my employees.*

The question posed by the advisor starts with the word "what" and is open ended. It is thought provoking and requires the client to provide more data to support her initial statement.

Step 3: The advisor reflects back what he has heard from the client to ensure accuracy.

Advisor: *What I hear you saying is you worry a lot about the business and making payroll and that is what is keeping you up at night.*

Client: *Yes. We are profitable, but I worry the other shoe will drop.*

Slowly the client is uncovering the different layers of her concern as the advisor asks more probing questions.

Step 4: The advisor demonstrates curiosity.

Advisor: *How will you know if the other shoe drops?*

Client: *I don't know. Seems kind of silly, doesn't it? But it was always something my dad used to say when he ran the company. That when things are going well, you better watch out because the other shoe might drop.*

Advisor: *Interesting. Tell me more.*

Client: *My dad was a perfectionist and very competitive. There was never enough revenue or success, and he worried a lot even when he had nothing to be anxious about. If I look at the numbers, our family business is doing great. We even make enough to reinvest some of the profits each quarter. But I still worry I am missing something.*

The advisor does not rush to problem solve, but instead asks clarifying questions to gather more insight into the client's experience.

Step 5: The advisor reflects back to the client what he has heard so far.

Advisor: *What I hear you saying is that you worry most about not making payroll, but the financial data indicates that you make enough for that and enough to reinvest in the company each quarter. Is that accurate?*

Client: *Yes. Sounds crazy, but I think he would want me to worry the way he did.*

This gives the client a chance to confirm the accuracy of the communication and correct any misinterpretation made by the advisor.

Step 6: The advisor summarizes the content and emotion of the communication and thanks the client for sharing.

> Advisor: *I appreciate your honesty and I don't think you are crazy. It seems like you want to honor your father, and worrying about the company is one way of doing it. This anxiety helps you stay on top of the business, but it also causes you to lose sleep.*
>
> Client: *Yes, that is exactly it.*
>
> Advisor: *If it is okay with you, maybe we could brainstorm other ways to stay on top of the business and honor your dad that involve your feeling better and sleeping more. What do you think?*
>
> Client: *That would be great.*

Notice how it is only when the advisor has a clear picture of what is going on with the client that he offers an opportunity to problem solve together.

To recap, active listening involves asking a general open-ended question at the beginning of the meeting and then letting the client determine the direction of the appointment. Each time the client offers information, the advisor asks clarifying questions until a mutual understanding is reached. At this time, the advisor summarizes what has been communicated, including any emotional content, and thanks the client for participating in the conversation. Then if necessary, the advisor works with the client, using more active listening, to determine possible solutions.

Active listening is really about you following the client's lead. While you may start the conversation with a question, the client decides what path to go down. It may be that she needs to talk about concrete data and financial information. Or she may want to discuss how her financial life feels in that moment. Either way, your job as a listener is to ask good questions, reflect back what you have heard, and validate her emotions. Instead of providing quick answers, you facilitate a discovery process that helps the client find her own answers. And when a client is part of the solution, she is more likely to follow through with the plan and view you as a valuable member of her financial team.

Roadblocks to Listening

Effective communication requires a commitment on your part. You need to practice the five skills involved in good communication regularly. You also need to be aware of and avoid some common roadblocks to effective client communication. These include mind reading, rushing, and thinking in black-and-white terms.

Mind Reading

Mind reading involves making assumptions about what your client is thinking and feeling and then taking action on these judgments without checking in to see if they are true. Typically, when you mind read you are coming up with statements and conclusions based on your values and beliefs. Because your upbringing, life experiences, and beliefs about money are probably not the same as your client's, reading her mind is a dangerous road to travel.

Similar to any long-term relationship, the familiarity with a client makes falling into this rut more likely. Think about the couples you

---

IN HER OWN WORDS

Money is such a personal thing, and as a rule women are not taught to understand how best to share this information. We often have different goals, often with children in mind, and applying the "normal" formulas will not work.

—KATHLEEN, WIDOW, 50 YEARS OLD WITH TWO CHILDREN

know who have been married for decades. Many of their conflicts stem from making assumption based on past experience as opposed to asking for current data. Be warned, if you have a long-term working partnership with a client, you may fall into the mind-reading trap. Over time, you can lose some of your curiosity, make faulty assumptions about what your client needs, and ask fewer questions. Your client may wonder why you seem to care less about her or are more likely to rush to problem solving than in the past. The challenge for you is that most clients won't directly express this concern; therefore, you need to notice when you are mind reading and make corrections accordingly.

To avoid this roadblock practice beginner's mind. Beginner's mind states that each time you have a conversation with a client, you pretend that it is your first. You let go of being an expert and allow the client to be an expert on herself. You stay curious and open to learning new things. All you have to do is spend time with a five-year-old child to be reminded of how to have beginner's mind. Toddlers view the world around them with wonder. Step into your child's or beginner's mind at the beginning of each meeting, and marvel at what you discover about your client.

My Way or the Highway

Another roadblock to good communication is approaching clients with the attitude that there is a right and a wrong way to save, spend, invest, and gift money. I call this the "my way or the highway" philosophy. It is a rigid way of thinking that professes that the path I am on when it comes to family values and managing money is the only road that is worthy. The dilemma with this approach is it does not factor in the complexities of coaching people with different cultures, personalities, values, and visions.

The "my way or the highway" mindset often plays out in subtle ways. For instance, do you ever find yourself leaving a client meeting shaking your head because she declined to follow your recommendations? Or have you ever made a judgment about how a client lives? Or maybe you only take on a client that has money habits similar to your own? While this is your prerogative, it may be a sign that you need to examine your openness to different ways of behaving and relating to people and wealth. The best part of working with clients is that everyone has a unique path. A competent and skilled advisor finds out what road the client is on and travels her highway during each meeting so he can best serve her.

To avoid practicing in a rigid, right-and-wrong way, let go of your preconceived notions about clients. Let your clients educate you on their rules of the road. Ask many questions and really listen to their answers. Remind yourself to bring your beginner's mind to your meetings with new as well as long-term clients. Follow the steps of active listening, and when you slip into a judgmental place, allow yourself to let go of being "right" and instead embrace what is "right" according to your client.

Hurry Up, Lady

If you are rushing through a meeting, it is almost impossible to be an effective communicator. Focusing on the clock, your agenda, and your next appointment distracts you from being present with the client in front of you. Most clients, especially female ones, can feel you rushing and are put off by your not allotting adequate time in your schedule for them. Rushing female clients is not good for business. It increases your stress level and deteriorates your clients' faith in you.

Are you saying, "But my schedule is so full, the market is crazy, and my boss is breathing down my neck"? I understand the demands on your time. I also appreciate that slowing down and really listening to each client is harder on some days than others. But it is a fact that clients are really put off by this behavior. The time you save cutting the appointment short probably will be spent prospecting for a new client later on.

Women are slower to hire financial advisors, take longer to make financial decisions, and share in more detail than men. Instead of racing the clock, simply schedule longer meetings. If the meeting ends earlier, use the extra time wisely. If the client needs the entire time, let her have it. As you get to know each client, you will be able to get a sense of the time she needs. Rick Harkins of Harkins Wealth Management specializes in advising women in transition. "What I have learned is to block off more time for certain female clients. This allows the client to take her time sharing information and is a great way to build a stronger relationship with her." Besides allowing her time to foster trust with you, the extra time in your schedule may help reduce your stress level as well.

Summary

The biggest complaint women have about financial advisors is that they don't listen. Therefore, it is your job to develop good communication skills and master the art of listening to better serve your female clients. For male advisors, this can be tricky as it goes against your male brain's desire to problem solve. Instead, you need to tap into your feminine side and actively listen. Validate her feelings, ask curious questions, and wait until she is ready to look at financial solutions. Practice all the tools of good communication, and know that if you pay attention to the "softer side" of finance, your female clients are more likely to trust you, be loyal to you, and make high-quality referrals.

Your Next Step: Building Your Listening Muscles

The only way to build your listening muscles is to practice. To do this, find a study partner and set aside 30 minutes to fully complete this exercise. Each partner will have 10 minutes to role-play the "advisor." After both of you have had a turn as the advisor, you will take the last 10 minutes to process the experience and put what you learned into action.

Start by deciding who will play the "advisor" and who will play the "client" in the first session. Set a timer for 8 minutes, then have the "advisor" initiate the dialogue by asking the client the following question: "What are you most proud of financially?" The advisor's goal is to actively listen to the client's answer and follow the active listening formula to gain a clear understanding of the client's answer. Keep the dialogue going until the time is up. Then take 2 minutes to answer the questions below in writing.

Advisor Questions

1. What was it like to actively listen to the client?

2. What insights did you gain about the client that you might have missed otherwise?

3. What did you learn about yourself as an advisor?

4. How can you use this insight to improve your active listening and communication skills with clients?

Client Questions

5. Using a scale of "1" (lowest) to "5" (highest), how well did the advisor listen?

6. Name one skill the advisor excelled at during the conversation.

7. Name one area for improvement and an idea about how to work on this skill.

Do not share your answers now. Instead, switch roles and repeat the exercise. Once you have both role-played each part, take the last 10 minutes to share your answers and discuss your experience as both the advisor and the client. After debriefing for 10 minutes, fill out the following as a way of taking action on improving your listening skills:

The action I will take to improve my listening skills is _____
_____.

I will complete this action step by _____, and my
accountability partner for this action step is _____
_____.

7

Fostering Financial Confidence

Confidence comes not from always being right,
but from not fearing being wrong.

—Peter T. McIntyre, artist and writer

Tina, 41 years old and single, shows up to your office early and impeccably dressed. She makes well over six figures in her high-powered sales management position and is looking for a new financial advisor. Tina is bright, articulate, and accomplished. She starts the consultation with a confession, "I am probably the worst client you have ever seen." Tina goes on to share that she has a retirement plan and investments and is working at reducing her spending. The more she tells you about her financial life, the more you think to yourself that this woman knows her stuff. So why does she feel like "such a mess" financially?

Tina, like many intelligent and capable women, suffers from low financial confidence. Her net-worth statement looks great, but her money-esteem is poor. While she is not perfect with her finances, she is financially literate and coachable. But inside she feels inadequate and underprepared to invest money and save for retirement.

135

However, with a little coaching and support from you, Tina can build her financial confidence and live more at peace with money.

What is financial confidence? Defining it is no easy task. It is a mix of basic financial know-how, a can-do attitude, and a belief in one's worth. It does not equate to making perfect decisions about money or always selecting the right investment. Financial confidence has more to do with trusting yourself to take some risks and knowing that you will mess up from time to time. It is learning what information you need to consider when making a financial decision and also how your personal values and money beliefs impact your choices. Financial confidence is not correlated with the amount of money you have, but with the comfort level you have in knowing you are doing your best every day to manage it.

As with self-esteem, financial esteem or confidence is not static. It shifts and changes over time in relation to a client's life circumstances and developmental challenges. Loss of a job, death of a parent or spouse, divorce, or a liquidity event can shake a client's belief in her ability to handle money and wealth responsibly. If the client has a solid foundation of confidence, then the dip into uncertainty is temporary and your role is to support her through this difficult time. If your female client is already operating at a low level of financial confidence, then these life events may require more from you in terms of education, patience, and hand-holding.

Women who are financially confident take charge of their financial lives and spend time and energy regularly managing their money. They teach their children and grandchildren how to be financially literate and allow them to learn from their mistakes. These women understand the mechanics of how to save, spend, invest, and gift wisely. While they are not necessarily experts in finance, they know the questions to ask and who to turn to for the answers. Financially confident women use the support of advisors, family, and friends, but ultimately take full responsibility for their decisions.

Unfortunately, many intelligent and accomplished women lack

financial confidence. The reason for this varies from person to person. For some it is not having enough practice at making financial decisions and for others it is not having the literacy to know what action to take. Low financial confidence contributes to women not practicing good self-care, overly relying on partners when it comes to financial matters, and often being fearful to seek out your professional guidance.

A Woman's Issue

Research shows that women lack financial confidence and tend to have a lower level of education and knowledge about investments and money management than men. Here are a few concerning statistics:

- 90 percent of women reported feeling insecure when it came to personal finance.[1]
- 48 percent of women agreed with the statement, "Investing is scary for me," which is twice the rate of men who answered this way.[2]
- Female clients' knowledge of annuities, mutual funds, and individual securities is limited.[3]
- Only one-third of affluent women reported being confident in their ability to meet their long-term financial goals, compared to half of their male counterparts.[4]

Why is there a gender gap when it comes to financial confidence? I believe it is a combination of lack of exposure to financial training and money management discussions, the societal bias against financially confident women, and the collective female tendency to underestimate self-worth.

Lack of Exposure

Historically, men were raised and educated to be wealth creators and providers for their families. Wealth was passed down to sons, with daughters receiving a smaller portion of the riches. Trusts, managed by male trustees, were created to help female inheritors, who were thought to lack financial skills and aptitude, manage their money. Once a woman found a suitable man to marry, the man took over the finances. While this may seem like a long time ago, a woman as the primary breadwinner, wealth creator, and manager of family wealth is still a relatively new concept. Couple the fact that women did not enter the workforce in a major way until the 1980s with a male-dominated financial services industry bent toward catering to men and it is no wonder women feel like fish out of water when it comes to investments and finance. Until recently, they have been!

In Her Own Words

My parents taught me that I am incompetent to manage my own money. Besides, if I managed my finances and the money grew and expanded, then I would not know what to do.
—NAN, *48 YEARS OLD, MARRIED INHERITOR, CURRENTLY UNEMPLOYED*

The lack of exposure to financial training and practice at managing money is part of the reason women lag behind in money-esteem. Socially, women are not expected or encouraged to talk about mutual funds, stocks, or bonds. Instead, women discuss relationships, family and friends, and the challenges of caregiving with others. Men more frequently discuss money. Think about the last dinner party you attended. What were the women discussing compared to the men? Chances are the female guests chatted about the latest recipe and gossip, and left the stock market tips to the men. While this may sound sexist, it is a cultural observation that can be seen time and time again. Some women are joining investment groups or forming money clubs to create an opportunity for them to openly talk about money and learn about finance. However, a woman's tendency to be less exposed socially to financial discussions can negatively impact her money-esteem.

Society's Bias

To further complicate matters, a woman with financial confidence is both admired and criticized in our society. Professional women who build successful businesses or have high-powered careers are looked up to as role models and also labeled as too aggressive, too money hungry, or not feminine. Powerful women, such as Hillary Rodham Clinton, Jennifer Aniston, and Oprah Winfrey are perfect examples of how women can be revered for having economic power and fortitude and simultaneously condemned as demanding and unpleasant to work with.

Women who marry into wealth don't get a break from this social taboo. These women are seen as gold diggers, trophy wives, or opportunists. Jokes are made behind their backs as to their motives for marrying their partners with little or no regard for the idea that they may actually be in love. If they take control of their finances, they are criticized for being too controlling. If they defer investment management to their husbands, they are seen as weak.

Female inheritors don't escape harsh judgment either. These women are often depicted as shopaholics who spend their days decorating and redecorating their homes or party girls who bounce from one red carpet event to the next. The popularity of reality television shows, such as *Keeping Up with the Kardashians* and *The Real Housewives of Beverly Hills*, does nothing but reinforce this stereotype.

The bottom line is that being a financially confident woman is a complicated proposition. Not only do you have to feel good about money, you have to have the self-worth to tolerate widespread disapproval by our society for being a woman who enjoys making and managing money.

Self-Doubt

From a very early age, girls are taught to downplay accomplishments as a way of fitting in and boys are taught to display overconfidence as a way of standing out. I witness the outcome of this firsthand when I conduct workshops for female attorneys and financial services professionals. It is striking to know how well-educated and talented these women are and to see how challenging it is for them to ask for money and referrals or accept praise. Their struggle is not unique. It sheds light on how overtly displaying confidence, financial or otherwise, requires a woman to swim against a strong societal undercurrent that is constantly telling her to play small.

This feminine tendency to share credit and deflect praise contributes to women having, or at least appearing to have, more self-doubt than men. In a 2011 study conducted by Europe's Institute of Leadership and Management, men felt that women displayed low self-confidence, which hurt their careers. While this may be more a matter of perception since men who boast are more socially acceptable than women who do, it does have negative consequences for women in general. In this survey, 70 percent of men reported high confidence levels, compared to only 50 percent of women. Women believe that their accomplishments should speak for themselves, resulting in many of them not going after promotions or competing for new positions. In fact, the study found that this lack of confidence contributed to a more cautious approach, with 20 percent of men applying for positions where they were only partially qualified, compared to only 14 percent of women doing the same.[5]

This self-doubt trickles down into a woman's entire financial life. Many of my female clients express that they don't know enough about investments to seek out the help of a financial advisor. It is very similar to the belief that you need to clean up for the maid. Somehow women think that they need to have their financial house in order to allow a professional to see it. But ultimately, this just keeps them stuck knowing less about money and having a lower level of financial confidence.

The best way to address this self-doubt is to lower the barriers of entry. By this, I mean making it easy and safe for women who are uncertain about their financial skills to connect with you. You need to be approachable and to normalize her experience. Telling stories about other clients whom you have worked with and how they came in to see you when they were feeling weary and a little uncertain regarding their money management skills can help. Also, consider hosting women's events that speak to the issue of female financial confidence. You can do this indirectly by sponsoring an event targeted at raising financially confident children. Chances are many of the mothers in the room want to spare their daughters (and sons) from feeling unprepared financially because the mother lacked financial preparedness training growing up.

In Her Own Words

I cannibalized my parents' money because I did not feel worthy of it.

—Barbara, 47 years old, married inheritor

No matter what the cause of low financial confidence, it negatively impacts female clients and needs to be addressed when you are working with them. It is important for you to recognize these women when they show up in your office and understand how to coach them toward financial mastery. These women may fear financial abandonment and suffer from bag lady syndrome, be financially overly dependent on a partner or parent, or lack the skills necessary to earn a competitive wage in the workplace. Let's take a look at each of these types of women and how you can boost their financial confidence.

Bag Lady Syndrome

Many women worry about ending up destitute and in the streets in their senior years. This is called "Bag Lady Syndrome" and often stems from lack of confidence in knowing how to make and manage money. Janet Acheatel, senior wealth manager and cofounder of Wealth by Design for Women, shares that even very affluent women can struggle with this issue. "I see a lack of financial confidence even with women who certainly have enough money. They still voice that fear of becoming a bag lady." For other women it may be a real financial concern that is overly exaggerated due to an unusually highly emotional relationship with money. The panic felt precludes these women from taking positive corrective action in their financial lives. The challenge for you is that female clients need a lot of emotional support before they can take action. While financial education needs to be part of the plan, first you need to explore her money scripts to uncover the source of her feelings.

A money script is a thought or belief about money and its purpose in the world. This script, similar to how a movie script instructs an actor what to say and feel in a scene, tells you how to behave in a particular financial situation. The sum of all of your money scripts is called your money mindset. Ultimately this money mindset dictates how you save, spend, invest, and gift daily. For instance, if every time you receive a bonus at work, you jump on the Best Buy website to buy the latest electronic gadget, you have a money script that says, "Bonuses are free money to spend on fun stuff." Or if you receive your bonus and immediately pay down your mortgage, your money script might be more like "Extra money, like a bonus, should go toward paying down debt." One money script is not right or wrong. But it does impact your financial habits.

Most of us are not aware of our money mindsets because these thoughts reside just below the surface in our unconscious mind. These money scripts were formed when we were young and observing our parents and other influential adults interact and talk (or not talk) about money. Because these messages form in our child's mind, they are often overly simplistic and not sufficient to capture the complexity of adult money management. Furthermore, some money beliefs are very black and white and some are overgeneralized and trigger bad feelings about money and ourselves.

To work on a woman's financial confidence, start by helping her uncover her money scripts and determine which ones contribute to her fears about her future. By bringing these thoughts and beliefs to the surface, she can then decide to keep the existing script or to alter it to make it more useful in taking care of her finances. Here are some questions to ask her to get the conversation started:

♦ What is the purpose of money and wealth?
♦ What is your biggest fear regarding your financial future, and what factors contribute to your believing this will be your fate?
♦ At what age did you start to worry about your financial future?
♦ What has retirement looked like for the women in your family?
♦ What would you like your retirement years to look like?
♦ What, if anything, needs to change for you to be less anxious about this next phase of your life?

Whether her fear of becoming financially destitute is real or an expression of her feeling of financial insecurity, it is important for you to show empathy and validate her experience. Too often, advisors make well-intentioned statements, such as "See on this spreadsheet, you have more than enough money, so you don't need to worry," that alienate the client and do nothing to alleviate her concerns. Instead of making a financial case to reduce her anxiety, learn more about her feelings. It may be that a money script passed down for generations is tripping her up. Or her anxiety may be the only way she can ask for your help in taking a more active role in her financial life. Whatever the cause, the solution starts with asking her questions and listening to the answers. In time, she will be ready to move into action. But if you problem solve too soon, you lose the opportunity to help her build insight into her relationship with money and wealth that eventually will allow her to address her bag lady syndrome head on.

Financial Dependency

Financial dependency is defined as putting your financial well-being in the hands of others to your own detriment. It involves someone, usually a parent or a spouse, enabling you not to take adult responsibility for money.[6] As you know, the trouble with financial dependency is that it leaves women vulnerable and unprepared for the time when the enabler leaves or passes on. The dilemma is that many of these women do not see it as a problem and/or are married to men who prefer them to be dependent. This does not mean you can't help these women increase their financial skills and confidence, just that it is often a slower process.

The financially dependent woman is the client you seldom see in your office. If she does show up, often at your request, she is quiet during the meeting. As one wealth manager shared with me, "Sometimes you have to guess at what would be in her best interest. You try to invite her to the meetings and politely ask her husband to allow her to share her input, but with little success." More likely, the financially dependent woman shows up in your office crying after her husband leaves her for a younger woman or after he suddenly dies of a heart attack. While this is not ideal, it is an opportunity for you to help her examine her overreliance on others financially and encourage her to build enough financial confidence to be an active participant in her financial life.

Women currently in their sixties and seventies tend to be more financially dependent than those from younger generations. These individuals were raised at a time when the cultural expectation was for them to get married, raise children, and let their husbands worry about money. With the feminist movement in the 1960s and women entering the workforce in the 1970s and 1980s, the expectation has shifted, but only slightly. Now women in their twenties choose a career over getting married. They become professionally established and live independently until they are ready to settle down. However, many of these women are still not taking full responsibility for their finances as evidenced by overspending and undersaving. Some even receive financial assistance from their parents well into their adult years.

IN HER OWN WORDS

I just want to be able to spend money and not worry about it. We have more than enough, so why do I need to balance my checkbook or set a limit on my spending? I just want to be carefree.
—CHARLENE, 37-YEAR-OLD MARRIED INHERITOR AND STAY-AT-HOME MOTHER OF THREE

Why are women prone to financial dependency? One reason is that our society teaches little girls, even in today's girl empowerment culture, that Mr. Right will take care of them financially. Fairy tales such as *Cinderella* and *Sleeping Beauty*, while appearing harmless, reinforce the message that someday Prince Charming will ride in on his white horse and rescue them. Not only will he love them but he will give them the life of a Princess. The last time I checked, Princesses in fairy tales were not paying bills, funding retirement accounts, or diversifying their stock portfolio. I am not against fairy tales, but wouldn't it be great if they were balanced out with stories of empowered women who live as financial equals with their men? Sometimes Prince Charming comes with debt, alimony payments, a gambling problem, or a weak heart. And when this happens, the Princess needs to step up and take over the kingdom.

Financially dependent women can be an advising challenge. They don't necessarily want to build financial confidence or learn about money. But as an advisor you have a responsibility to serve your clients well. This means if she is a partner in a couple, her needs must be considered too. Here are some practical steps you can take to connect and help a financially dependent female client.

First, consider meeting with her individually. This allows you to talk with her privately about your concerns and to start building a connection with her. As already mentioned, a large percentage of widows transfer their assets from the couple's advisor to a new one shortly after the death of the spouse. Simply by taking the time to get to know her, you are in a better position to help her when and if a crisis comes up that requires her to step up to the plate and take the lead in her financial life.

Next, consider talking with the couple about the pros and cons of having one person in the couple oversee all aspects of their financial life. Do this in a way that is nonjudgmental and respectful. Ask curious, open-ended questions to understand more about how the couple operates and how this mode of operation may be useful and also how it may be problematic. Here are some questions to consider asking both members of the couple:

◆ What did your parents teach you about how couples manage money and wealth?
◆ What is the advantage of your deferring financial decisions and planning to your partner?
◆ What are the disadvantages of your deferring financial decisions and planning to your partner?
◆ What message do you think your current way of interacting with money and wealth sends your children or grandchildren?
◆ What, if anything, would you be willing to do differently so that both of you could be prepared if the other were no longer here to make decisions?

By raising these questions with couples, you are allowing both spouses to consider the positive and negative impact of the wife's financial dependency. This increased awareness may be all you are able to do before a life event shifts the couple dynamic. But even though short-term change is not evident, it does lay the foundation for working with her in the future. Also, she might surprise you and decide she does want to be more involved. Maybe she was just waiting to be asked.

Underearning

Women who underearn have low financial confidence that causes them to tolerate making less than they are worth. These women, according to Barbara Stanny, author of *Overcoming Underearning*, can be affluent because underearning has to do not with the amount of money you have or make but with the attitude you have about your worth.[7]

At the beginning of my career in wealth psychology, I worked with hundreds of women who underearned. These women were bright, creative, and energetic. But they all lacked the belief in their monetary worth and their ability to negotiate fees and salaries. The assumption many of these women made is that they were lucky to have a job, and the boss will compensate them more as long as they do good work. This is a big part of the reason that women still earn only 77 cents to every man's dollar.[8] We are not asking for the full dollar. As you know from working in financial services, it is rare to make more money unless you have the confidence and skills to ask.

In the book *Women Don't Ask*, the authors, Linda Babcock and Sara Laschever, share some startling statistics:[9]

- Men initiate a salary negotiation four times more than women.
- 20 percent of adult women (approximately 22 million women) NEVER negotiate, even though they think it is a good idea.

◆ Women expect less when negotiating and as a result receive 30 percent less than men when negotiating.

What this equates to is women don't have the financial esteem to ask for more and as a result get less.

Helping women overcome underearning is an area where you can really make a difference. If you are a male advisor, you probably have a more positive mindset about negotiating and more experience successfully advocating for your worth. If you are a female advisor, you probably are more confident than most women without your financial expertise. Either way, you make a perfect mentor for underearning female clients.

In Her Own Words

Once I understood money, it changed so much for me. It changed how I felt about myself. I felt more confident, powerful, and self-sufficient. It even changed how I developed relationships, such as dating and friendships.

—BRENDA, *47 YEARS OLD, DIVORCED MOTHER OF THREE STEPCHILDREN*

AND ENTREPRENEUR

Start by asking your clients about their money scripts relative to asking for and receiving money. Often these women believe it is rude to ask for money or not ladylike. Consider asking the following questions to explore their attitudes toward negotiation:

◆ What is your worth in the marketplace?
◆ Do you think people will pay you that amount? Why or why not?
◆ What do you think of women who ask for more money or for bonuses?

◆ What were you taught growing up about negotiating?

◆ When was the last time you negotiated for money? What were you thinking and feeling? What was the outcome?

Once you determine the money scripts that are blocking a woman from earning more, it is time to practice. Role-play a negotiation with her in your office. Play both roles so you can model good negotiation skills and also give her a chance to fine-tune her own. Remind her that she negotiates in other areas of her life every day. What woman doesn't negotiate with her family constantly? Who is picking up the kids after school? Who is buying the milk on the way home from work? Who is helping Johnny with his homework? Women know how to negotiate, they just need to learn to transfer those skills to negotiating for money.

Next, agree to be her mentor. Sometimes women need to talk through a potential negotiation before it happens. Invite her to call you if she needs to brainstorm about an upcoming meeting, and serve as her mentor both inside and outside the office. In time, her financial confidence will grow, she will learn how to effectively negotiate, and her earnings potential will skyrocket. Not only is this good for your client, but it is good for you since she will accumulate more wealth for you to manage.

Fostering Her Financial Confidence

As an advisor, there are many ways you can boost a female client's financial confidence. Some of these techniques have been discussed above. In an effort to make these tools accessible for you and your clients, I have developed a model called the ABCs of Fostering Financial Confidence. In this model, A stands for "Analyze," B for "Build," and C for "Coach." Each step is detailed below:

Analyze

The first step in the ABCs of Fostering Financial Confidence is to analyze your client's current level of financial intelligence. Financial intelligence is the sum of your financial literacy, your money skills, and your ability to understand what you think and feel about money and wealth. When you have a higher level of financial intelligence, you typically have a higher level of financial confidence. Women with low money-esteem have a deficit when it comes to one or more of these areas—financial knowledge, skill, or insight. Your job is to find out where her deficits lie and to develop a plan for building these areas.

The following is an assessment tool for evaluating your client's level of financial knowledge, money skill, and insight into her relationship with money.

Financial Confidence Assessment

Please answer the following questions. There are no "right" or "wrong" answers to these questions. Please be as open and honest in your responses and know that everyone has a different experience and skill level when it comes to money and investments.

Your Financial Knowledge

1. What did your parents and family teach you about managing money as a child?
2. What financial education, formal or otherwise, have you had to date?
3. On a scale from "1" to "5" with "1" being the least, rate your current level of financial literacy.
4. What makes you a _____ (fill in your number here) versus a "5"?
5. What number would you like to be?

Your Money Skills

6. How often do you balance your checkbook and savings accounts?

7. Do you have a spending plan and if so, how often do you review it? Are you able to follow it, and if not, why?

8. Do you read and review your investment reports? Why or why not?

9. Are you familiar with the various types of investment vehicles, such as equities, bonds, annuities, and mutual funds?

10. On a scale of "1" to "5," with "1" being the least, rate your current ability to negotiate money.

Your Financial Insight

11. How would you describe your relationship with money and wealth?

12. What values and beliefs do you have about money and its purpose in your life?

13. When you make financial decisions, what motivates you to act the way you do?

14. What thoughts trigger you to spend money? Save money? Invest money?

15. What would you like to teach the next generation about money and wealth?

The answers to these questions provide information on your client's financial competence and money scripts. Discuss the answers with her, and collaborate on developing a plan for addressing those areas of her financial intelligence that could use some strengthening. You are now ready to move to the building phase.

Build

The second step in the ABCs for Fostering Financial Confidence is "B," which stands for building knowledge, skills, and insight through education, discussion, and support. After you have analyzed and discussed the areas for improvement with your client, it is time for you and her to come up with an agreed-upon approach to increasing her confidence. Make sure you factor in her preferred learning style, and follow up with her regularly. Be as creative and collaborative as possible during the building phase because often clients have wonderful ideas on addressing their problems. The process of deciding together also enhances the advisor-client bond and shows her that you are invested in her taking care of herself financially.

Here are a few suggestions on how to build financial confidence based on the client's area of need. When designing a plan, make sure it gives her permission to take baby steps toward changing her relationship with money. Support her in taking small steps since setting up a plan that is too big can be overwhelming. The best route for long-term positive gains in financial intelligence and money-esteem is to build the blocks of confidence one brick at a time.

Knowledge-Building Tools

- Encourage her to read the book *Women's Worth: Finding Your Financial Confidence* by Eleanor Blayney, CFP. This book is written for women who are interested in learning more about the mechanics of finance. It is easy to read, contains case examples, and offers practical tips for taking action.
- For women in their thirties, the book *On Your Own Two Feet: A Modern Girl's Guide to Personal Finance*, written by two financial experts Manisha Thakor and Sharon Kedar, is a good resource. It is a small, manageable book broken into digestible sections that make learning about money, investing, and saving for retirement fun. While older women can enjoy it too, it has a young hip vibe that lends itself to a younger audience.

◆ Refer her to financial literacy websites. These include the Women's Institute for Financial Education, Learn Vest, and Daily Worth. Refer to The Female-Friendly Resource Guide at the back of this book for web addresses and details.

◆ Encourage her to meet with you to develop a financial literacy program for her children or grandchildren. As you put together the protocol, discuss different financial terms and concepts as a way of empowering her to acquire the knowledge to pass down to the next generation.

Skill-Building Tools

◆ Teach her the mechanics of balancing a checkbook or reading an investment report. This may be an easy task for you as an advisor, but for her it could be the first time someone has taken the time to teach her these skills.

◆ Use role-plays to help her build her skills in negotiating and talking about money. Act out different scenarios so she can be more prepared when she is actually asking for money.

◆ Select a handful of women from your practice who need help building money skills, and ask them to meet regularly at your office. At each meeting pick a topic for discussion, such as saving for retirement, reading financial statements, or creating a realistic spending plan. Keep the meetings informal, and allow adequate time for conversation and interplay between the members.

Insight-Building Tools

◆ Give her a copy of my workbook *Creating Wealth from the Inside Out: A Step-by-Step Guide for Changing How You Think and Feel About Money*. This book takes the reader through a simple three-step process to help her uncover her money scripts, gain insight into her relationship with money, and take action toward healthier financial habits. This workbook is best used in conjunction with some meetings with you where the material can be discussed and integrated into her financial plan.

◆ If overspending and shopping is an issue, consider giving her the book *To Buy or Not to Buy: Why We Overshop and How to Stop* by April Lane Benson, PhD. Ask her to read a chapter or two between regular meetings and encourage her to e-mail or bring in questions at your next appointment.

◆ Encourage her to work with a wealth psychology consultant or a financial therapist as a way to better understand her relationship with money. A good consultant coordinates the learning with you and provides your client additional emotional support.

Once you decide on a course of action, it is time for the last part of the ABCs of Fostering Financial Confidence. It is time for "C," to coach her.

Coach

Coaching is a key element in building a woman's financial confidence. As with all new things, it takes time and practice to integrate knowledge, skill, and insight into your life. Therefore, your female clients need your coaching and guidance along the way.

To be a good coach you need to be part cheerleader, part teacher, and part mentor. You need to hold her accountable for what she promises to do and examine what happens when she does not follow through. You need to be nonjudgmental, respectful, and accepting. At the same time, you need to challenge her to go beyond the status quo. Don't give up if her progress is slow. Change takes time, and a good coach appreciates this and makes space for his client's imperfections in the learning and growing process.

Summary

Many women lack financial confidence and need your help to feel more comfortable making and managing money. As a knowledgeable financial advisor, you can boost your client's financial-esteem through education, discussions, and support. Make sure you do not assume all women need this type of help; instead, carefully assess each female client's level of financial confidence. When appropriate, work with her to develop a plan of action that includes increasing her concrete financial knowledge, money skills, and insights into her financial attitudes and behaviors. By supporting her in this way, not only will you foster increased financial confidence but you will also build trust and loyalty.

Your Next Step: Stepping Outside Your Comfort Zone

Chances are since you are reading this book and working in financial services you are financially confident. Therefore, it may be difficult to understand what it feels like for a woman who is struggling with low money-esteem. This coaching exercise will help you get in touch with what it feels like to not be sure of yourself and to have to make some decisions when you are feeling insecure.

Select an activity from the following list that is not in your area of expertise and something that you have very little experience doing:

____ Ordering wine from an extensive wine list in a French restaurant

____ Picking out fabric to sew a handmade garment or yarn to knit a baby sweater

____ Buying art supplies to paint a self-portrait

____ Playing a musical instrument, such as a piano, guitar, or violin

____ Cooking an upside-down cake

____ Other: [Fill in an activity of your own here]

_____

Once you have made your selection, set a date to try out this new activity. Notice what you think and feel while engaging in this new task. What does it feel like to make a decision based on having very little expertise or comfort level? What thoughts and feelings did you have when you stepped outside your comfort zone? What helped you complete the task? What did you learn about coaching someone else who is not confident by completing this activity? How can you use this information to help you coach women who are not financially confident?

8

Advising Women in Couples

*A long marriage is two people trying to dance a duet
and two solos at the same time.*

—Anne Taylor Fleming, journalist

ADVISING COUPLES IS AN ART, NOT A SCIENCE. IT REQUIRES AN UNDER-
standing of couple and family dynamics, and gender differences and
how to balance his needs with hers. As an advisor, you are required
to be part mediator, part facilitator, and part objective observer. You
can't take sides, even if you want to, and you need to keep your own
judgments and opinions as to how a couple should operate personally and financially out of the picture. Advising couples is challenging, but when done well is also rewarding and deeply satisfying.

There is very little written for financial services professionals on
how to effectively advise couples. This is surprising given the reality that most of the clients seen by financial advisors and planners
are couples. Advising and coaching couples is complex and at times
tricky because it is easy to unconsciously cater to one partner over
the other. Due to an industry bias and the reality that the majority
of financial advisors are men, the balance is often tipped toward the
male partner, leaving women feeling ignored and overlooked.

My belief is that you are doing your best to serve the couple and to find financial solutions that benefit both individuals. I don't believe you are purposely leaving women out of meetings and not factoring in her wishes during the advising process. Instead I think there is a longstanding expectation in the financial industry that the husband is the wealth creator, the decision maker, and the one with the power in the relationship. This is a societal myth that runs deep in our culture. When the Federal Reserve Bank, in a 2010 survey, asked who controls more private wealth in this country, 76 percent of Americans said men. These participants were shocked to learn that women were indeed in the majority at 51 percent, compared to men at 49 percent. This female majority is predicted to increase to 66 percent by 2030 due to women typically being double inheritors and the rapid growth of women-owned businesses resulting in more females than males accumulating wealth over the next few decades.[1] Because of this economic power misconception, there is an expectation and pattern in most firms to focus on the male client first and foremost. He is the one to please, to cater to, and to communicate with. And while historically this was accurate, it is no longer true.

This chapter offers ideas and strategies to assist you in avoiding the common mistakes made by well-intentioned advisors. These mistakes turn female clients off and ultimately end up contributing to them deciding to transfer their assets to the competition when they are in a position to do so. The changes suggested are easy to

---

IN HER OWN WORDS

I would call the advisor and he would call back my husband because that is who he saw as a more powerful person. He underestimated me totally. I have a lot of power behind the scenes.

—LUCY, 52-YEAR-OLD MARRIED BUSINESSWOMAN

implement and will make you a better advisor for all of your clients, including women.

Top Five Mistakes Advisors Make Working with Women in Couples

What are the common mistakes well-meaning advisors make when working with women in couples? Here are the top five according to the women and advisors I interviewed.

Mistake 1: Not Understanding Her Economic and Decision-Making Power in the Partnership

One of the biggest errors I see financial advisors make is not appreciating the woman's influence on the couple. This starts at the first meeting and typically continues throughout the engagement. Ted McLyman, CEO of Apexx Behavioral Solutions Group and author of *Money Makes Me Crazy*, shared his observations: "I can't tell you the number of young advisors that I have who spend an hour and a half with a new client couple and they think it went great. They spent 90 percent of their time talking to the guy and they validated all the sports metaphors and who did what, who did this, and the couple never comes back." Because what happened is when the couple went to the car, the female of the couple turned to the male and said, "That guy's a jerk, I don't care what you say, we're never going back." It is not only junior financial advisors who make this error. Ann Hughes, founder of The Female Affect, has witnessed this happening with both male and female advisors with years of experience. The mindset is: "They need to win over the male part of the equation, or they are not going to get them as clients." According to Hughes, some advisors throw in the towel on connecting with the female member of the couple before they get started, stating that they don't think they can win over the woman so they won't even try. This industry bias results in an alarmingly high number of women mistrusting advisors and becoming very dissatisfied consumers. With women making more than 80 percent of the buying decisions in the family, including whom to hire as a financial advisor, this is a costly mistake for you to make.[2]

Mistake 2: Not Including Her in All the Financial Discussions and Decisions

The next mistake financial advisors tend to make is not including her in all the financial discussions and decisions. While meeting with and communicating with only one member of a couple is less time consuming and often easier, it is not a good practice in the long run. The female client ends up left out of key decisions and an inactive participant in her financial life, both of which are far from ideal for her and for your advisor-client relationship. The dilemma is that some couples agree, either silently or overtly, to have the male partner be the sole decision maker and participant in your work. This is seen most often with older couples who are from a generation who believed managing and investing money was man's work. The risk of not including her in the financial planning meetings is high. If he passes first, she is ill-equipped to manage the family finances. She has little or no relationship with you, so the risk of her moving her assets elsewhere is extremely high.

Financial advisors vary on how strict they are in requiring couples to meet together. Christine Moriarty, CFP, founder of MoneyPeace, will not meet with one member of the couple alone. "You lose out on two accounts. One, creating a relationship with the nonparticipatory spouse and two, setting up a plan that the couple can 'buy into' and maintain." Other advisors will agree to meet with one partner, depending on the circumstances.

My recommendation is to educate your couples as to the many advantages of meeting, planning, and monitoring their financial lives together. These include designing a financial plan and investment strategy that works for both partners, working together to achieve these goals and objectives, and having a place to meet to periodically discuss money together with a neutral facilitator. Once the benefits of this model are explained, many couples agree to actively participate in advisor meetings. Remember if the couple has a long-standing pattern of the female client not participating, you may need to explain your rationale for wanting to meet with both partners more than once. If the client does not agree or refuses to include his wife, then it is up to you to determine if you can fulfill your fiduciary responsibility to the couple by meeting only with him.

Mistake 3: Misinterpreting Her Silence

A woman's silence in a meeting is commonly misinterpreted as her agreement with what is being said or as disinterest. However, women tend to be quiet when they are learning. As discussed in Chapter 2, "The Psychology of Women and Wealth," the female learning style tends to be more passive than active. Therefore, if your female client is quiet, it may be a more accurate indicator of her taking in new information than necessarily agreeing with what is being said. If she is silent for a large portion of the meeting, check in and find out what she is thinking and feeling about the information being discussed. It will give her a chance to voice her opinion, which some female clients need permission to do, and to give you the important information you need so you can either proceed with or revisit a concept.

Silence can also mean that she is deferring to her husband out of respect. One woman explained "When I'm physically out with my husband and it's about finances, it would be almost disrespectful to him in a way, because it's his field, if I was the one who was more vocal. That's how I always looked at it. So I talk to him privately about what I want and I let him be the public person." If this is the case for a couple you advise, you may want to consider setting up an individual appointment with the female client to give her an opportunity to voice her thoughts comfortably.

Mistake 4: Unintentionally Talking Down to Her

Female clients complain time and time again about financial advisors talking down to them. Statements such as "Don't worry your pretty little head about it" are reiterated as they roll their eyes. And even if you are not uttering these exact words, it may be what she hears. You need to be careful in telling a woman not to worry or to feel a certain way, or that the situation is complicated, but you will handle it for her. Often advisors think they are helping a female client by reassuring her that she does not need to be anxious, and instead it alienates her. The best strategy is to partner with her and validate her feelings. Find out what is causing the fear, and reframe it as "important information," not something to be squelched or dismissed. By doing so, you are showing her that you care, that her input is valuable, and that together you can find solutions to her unique financial situation.

IN HER OWN WORDS

A female client will likely be very loyal to you if she feels you are paying attention and respecting her wishes. She must feel comfortable asking questions and not feel that she is being talked down to because she is a woman.

—*KATHY, 57 YEARS OLD, DIVORCED, PSYCHOTHERAPIST*

One advisor told a story of a widow who just lost her husband and had about $3 million of investible assets from life insurance payments and investments. She had an adolescent daughter to care for and was just terrified that she was going to run out of money now that her husband was deceased. From the advisor's perspective, she was very financially responsible and her fears were unfounded. His first instinct was to show her the numbers and explain how she had enough money to fund college and support herself for life. However, he decided to take another route and partner with her in her worry. He said, "Your concern is incredibly healthy. It's making sure that you don't run out of money. So the first thing that we should do is just really take a moment and appreciate how valuable this concern is. At the same time, this concern might be eating away at you in a way that it doesn't need to, so let's also look at ways you can be more at peace and content around money while keeping the responsible aspect of this concern." This statement allowed the widow to be right in her feelings and to see it as both a strength as well as an area to work on. Prior to this meeting the advisor did not have any real relationship with the widow; however, his strength-based approach and collaborative style resulted in her working with him for many years after this discussion.

Mistake 5: Making Assumptions About Her Based on Gender Only

This mistake may seem contradictory since this book is about advising women and highlights key gender differences throughout the text. However, generalities about gender are helpful starting points, but they should not be used to categorize female clients into neat little homogeneous groups. For example, my husband and I do not fit the gender stereotype. He is not the dominant partner in financial meetings. Instead, I tend to do most of the talking because I am more familiar with the industry and he prefers to take a more laid back, secondary position in the meetings. This dynamic works for us as a couple and our advisor works with it nicely. However, in the past, advisors have pigeonholed me as the quiet, less financially educated spouse. This failure to really get to know me and to know us as a couple ultimately caused us to find a more female-friendly advisor.

Be careful: use gender differences as a starting point but not the end-all, be-all in your work with women. For example, as a whole, women are less financially literate than men, but individually they have varying degrees of financial know-how. Instead of assuming that your client has limited financial knowledge, take the time to check in with her and ask about her level of financial literacy. An easy way to do this is to have each member of the couple rate their financial know-how on a scale from "1" to "5," with "1" being the lowest of financial literacy and "5" being the highest. Keep in mind women tend to underestimate their abilities, whereas men overrate their competence. Use these self-reported ratings to determine how to present information in meetings. Directly discuss with both partners what type of financial education they want as part of the engagement and what level of detail or technicality they want you to use. Also take the time to get to know each female client as a unique human being by inquiring about her communication preferences, money values, and risk-tolerance level. By investing part of your meeting time in learning about her as an individual, you are demonstrating that you are female friendly and won't fall into the trap of making broad assumptions based solely on gender.

Now that you know the five most common mistakes advisors make while working with women in couples, what action can you take to avoid these pitfalls? The first step is raising your awareness regarding these common errors and noticing when you unintentionally fall into one of these traps. Next, you need to gain a basic understanding of couple dynamics and learn practical strategies for engaging both partners in the advising relationship.

One Plus One Equals Three

In math class you learned that $1 + 1 = 2$. But when you are advising couples, the answer is $1 + 1 = 3$. Yes, there are three entities in the room—the couple, and two individual adults. In other words, the sum of a couple's parts does not equal the whole. Instead you have individuals who, when together as a couple, impact each other with every decision they make or every action they take. A good analogy is a hanging mobile. The separate pieces of a mobile hang down and are perfectly balanced, with each one interconnected to the other. When you move one piece, there is a ripple effect through the entire system, making it impossible to move one part without moving the other. The same is true for couples. They are a system of at least two separate individuals. When one moves or takes action, there is a ripple effect through the system and the other one is impacted. Add children into the system and you have many interconnected moving parts to contend with.

Take a moment and think about your individual financial goals. Assume for a minute you are single with no family, no children, no parents, and no friends. How would you invest your money? How would you spend it? What would you do with your wealth when you died? Now add back your family and friends to the scenario. How does being a member of a couple or a family change your financial goals? Chances are, pretty dramatically because with every decision you make and every goal you establish, someone else in the system is being tossed around a bit.

In addition to understanding that you are working with three entities, it is also important to realize that couples, and in fact all family systems, resist change. A husband and wife may say they want to spend less, but at the next quarterly meeting have the same negative cash flow as before. A nontraditional couple may tell you that drafting an estate plan is a top priority for them, but fail to follow through with your referral. The reason? Couples crave homeostasis.

Do you remember the term *homeostasis* from high school science class? It refers to the desire for an organism to live in equilibrium. Just like any other living organism, a couple (or a family) works to keep their system in balance. Think about how many savers are married to spenders. This is a great way for a couple to stay balanced. If the overshopping partner decides to get help and decrease his spending, then watch out for the saver to start spending more. Often this rebalancing is not conscious on the part of the couple. However, it can make your job as a financial advisor frustrating because the words uttered in your office don't always match the behaviors outside the room. Noticing the disconnection between a couple's words and their actions can be helpful in facilitating change for them. It brings the behaviors to conscious thought, which makes it easier for the couple to act differently going forward. This type of noticing is not a guarantee of behavioral change, but it does pave the way for the possibility of new ways of interacting with money.

Homeostasis can be healthy or unhealthy, depending on the couple's overall ability to function. For example, take the Sopranos, the mob family depicted in the popular HBO series by the same name. This family is led by a very unhappy and unhealthy couple, Tony and Carmela. Violence, disrespect, infidelity, and poor money management abound. Their homeostasis keeps them stuck in unhealthy and often criminal patterns of behavior. Now consider the family from the popular 1970s show, *The Waltons*. Ma and Pa Walton work together to teach their children right from wrong and make the family work as a team. Their relationships and family, while not perfect, exemplify a well-balanced family system that is good for the individuals as well as for the family as a whole.

Understanding and appreciating a couple's natural tendency to gravitate toward homeostasis is helpful. It highlights why it is vital to have both partners present for the meetings and planning sessions. Real change is only going to occur in a couple when both members are willing and motivated to change. If the female client is left out of the dialogue, it is hard to know if she is on board or not.

Realizing that couples crave homeostasis is also helpful in reducing your frustration level. Some couples cannot operate any other way, so you can let go of trying to save couples like the Sopranos. And when you are working with clients who are healthy enough to take steps toward a healthier financial future, know that progress will be slow and reverting to old behaviors is to be expected. For example, a couple may agree to both be present for all financial appointments and then fail to attend the next meeting together. Your job is to respect that change takes time and to hold the couple accountable for their joint decision to attend together by rescheduling. Do this gently since your clients are acting like they always have as a couple and may need you to help them practice a new way of relating to each other around money. Just like the hanging mobile, the couple will eventually adopt new habits and will come back into balance after a while.

To be an effective advisor for couples, you need to appreciate the dynamics of couples and the need for homeostasis. You also have to decide how you want to work with couples and how you plan on factoring in each individual's different communication, learning, and interpersonal style. Let's now look at a few strategies that address these areas.

Strategies to Maximize Your Effectiveness with Couples

Now that you know a little bit more about couple dynamics, let's explore some strategies for minimizing difficult situations and maximizing your effectiveness with couples.

Strategy 1: Decide On Your Mode of Operation When Working with Couples

It is important that you decide how you plan on working with couples and then follow this protocol consistently. Some advisors require both partners to be present at all meetings and only communicate with both members. E-mails are copied to each partner and written correspondence is addressed to both parties. The rationale behind this service model is to minimize misunderstandings and avoid the appearance of aligning with one spouse over the other. It also ensures that all parties are up to date and in the decision-making loop.

Other advisors' service model is less rigid. The advisor meets regularly with the more financially dominant spouse, who is self-selected by the couple and often the male client. Periodically the female client is invited to check in, but these appointments are optional. Most communication happens unilaterally. This more traditional service model is most likely to result in your female clients feeling left out or, worse yet, neglected in the advising relationship.

Other practitioners combine approaches and meet with the couple in the first meeting, then with each partner individually to gather a more detailed data on each person's financial upbringing and individual financial goals. Subsequently, they encourage meetings with both members of the couple present. The idea behind the individual meetings is to develop a more solid relationship with each partner and also to attain information that each partner may not be as forthcoming with when meeting jointly.

The mode of operation is yours to decide. However, it is vital that you consciously decide how you would like to practice and then stick to this service model throughout the engagement. If you want to empower your female clients, I strongly recommend you encourage both partners to be present at all meetings. Joint communication allows each person to actively participate in the couple's decision making and also communicates to the couple that you care about both of them. Furthermore, it minimizes the likelihood of getting caught in the middle of the couple when disagreements about financial and life planning arise.

Strategy 2: Be Transparent and Consistent in How You Work with the Couples

Once you have selected your couple's service model, be consistent in the implementation. Educate couples in your first meeting about how you work with couples and your rationale for practicing this way. By explaining your methodology up front and being transparent about your philosophy, couples can self-select to work with you or not.

As the advisor-client relationship matures, there may be times you need to reinforce your service model. While you may have a tendency to make an exception, it is best to adhere to your original plan. If you explained your philosophy previously, rescheduling or postponing an appointment due to only one partner showing up generates a less negative push back from the couple. Instead, holding them accountable to work on their financial lives together is more likely to be viewed as helpful and caring. Don't forget that technology makes this goal more practical now that one partner can attend by telephone or Skype if necessary.

Strategy 3: Keep the Triangle Balanced Inside and Outside the Office

When you are advising couples there are three people, or a triad, in each meeting. As you know, you need to balance the conversation and interaction with each member of the couple during appointments. This can be challenging, especially if one partner is more verbal than the other or if you naturally connect with one person more than the other. As Kol Birke, financial behavior specialist with Commonwealth Financial Network, says, "Make sure you balance the triangle because when you focus most of your energy on one client, it tips the triangle in their direction and the other client can end up feeling ignored."

Refer to Figure 8.1. You are at the top of the triangle and a husband and a wife are at the other two axis points. The two lines connecting you to the two other points represent your relationship with each of the individuals. The line between the husband and wife represents the dynamic between the couple. When in balance, each individual is participating in the interaction and getting his or her needs met. When the triangle is out of balance, as shown in Figure 8.1, one spouse is being left out of the conversation. If the dialogue is out of balance too frequently, then one spouse may feel ignored or neglected by you, whether intentional or not.

Figure 8.1

Balancing the Conversation with Couples

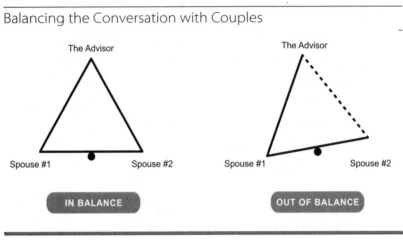

In a typical meeting, the triangle occasionally tips from one side to the next, but it should never be out of balance for too long. Check in with yourself two or three times throughout the meeting and ask "Is the triangle in balance?" If it is, then consciously redirect the conversation or questioning to the other partner.

This triangle also needs to be kept in balance outside the office as well. If you play golf with him, play tennis with her. If she e-mails you with a question, respond by hitting "reply to all" and include him on the correspondence. While these actions may seem tiny and unimportant, they have a big impact on your work with couples and on building trust with your female clients.

Strategy 4: Practice Good Self-Management and Get into the Client's Mindset

Self-management refers to the ability to put your personal interest and opinions aside, and focus solely on what is important and relevant to the client. Good self-management comes from knowing what your thoughts, beliefs, and attitudes are toward money, wealth, and couplehood. It is practicing in a client-centric fashion, even when your personal beliefs conflict with your client's. Good self-management requires you to acknowledge your bias and remain focused on your client's wishes.

Part of self-management is being aware of your tendency to cater to the client who is paying your bill. You have a fiduciary responsibility to the couple, but may find yourself reluctant to confront an aggressive wealth creator in a meeting because he or she writes the check. Remember she is just as important in the advisor-client relationship, even more so in the long run because she is likely to be your client the longest. Notice this and other tendencies to align with one partner over the other, and then do not act on them.

Strategy 5: Put Yourself in Your Client Couple's Shoes and Validate Their Feelings

Financial services professionals generally are "fix-it" people with great analytical and problem-solving skills. When working with couples, it is important to be able to put yourself in your client couple's shoes, which is a different skill set. This type of advanced client communication skill is rarely taught in graduate or training programs in financial services and, if so, is not part of the required curriculum. Therefore, it can be challenging for an advisor to appreciate that, even though a couple has millions of dollars, the wife is still worried about running out of money or that the husband, a multimillionaire, is still working at 70 years of age even though he tells you at every meeting he wants to retire. On paper these concerns are unfounded. But in a client's mind, they are very real.

The good news is learning how to step into your client's shoes is a very teachable skill, but in order to do so, Birke explains that you must let go of the need for your clients to be rational. "I would say that the advisors who accept that all humans (including their clients) think and act emotionally/irrationally are the ones that are most able to figure out what their clients need in order to move forward." A client-centered advisor does not judge a couple's beliefs and values about money, but instead works to understand them. Through active listening and exploration, find out what motivates your clients to think and feel the way they do. Ask the affluent wife mentioned above how much money it would take not to fear becoming financially destitute. Inquire about where this thought came from and how it might help her when it comes to spending, saving, and investing. Remember, what makes working with couples interesting is that everyone has his or her own financial mindset. Your job is not to pass judgment and make their mindset align with yours. Instead, you are tasked with understanding each partner's mindset and developing a financial plan that honors and incorporates these beliefs and values.

The next time you are baffled by a client couple, take a step back and put yourself in the couple's shoes. Let go of any "shoulds" or right and wrong judgments. Instead, ask curious questions to learn more about your client's mindset. Use this information to appreciate your client's situation and how you can tailor a solution to meet their mindset, not yours.

Strategy 6: When in Doubt, Consult

When working with couples, it is important to recognize what you know and what you do not know. You can get pulled into acting in ways that are not in line with your service model. This has nothing to do with your competence; it is because working with couples and families is complicated. If you notice that you are not following your protocol or you are spending too much time thinking about a particular couple, consider consultation. Talking about an advising situation with a trusted colleague or a consultant with expertise in couple and family dynamics is not only good for you, but for the couple you are advising.

If you are looking for a wealth consultant or couples counselor in your area to consult with, network with your colleagues to find a good referral. Also consider visiting the Financial Therapy

Association website at http://www.financialtherapyassociation.org, the website for the Family Firm Institute at http://www.ffi.org, or check out the local chapter of the American Association of Marriage and Family Therapy at http://www.aamft.org.

As you can see, advising couples involves a delicate balance of attending to his and her needs and being aware of your biases. The aforementioned strategies will help you maximize your effectiveness advising both traditional and nontraditional couples.

Attending to Her Needs

What extra steps can you take to make sure your female client feels included and valued when you are advising her as a member of a couple? Here are some practical tips that address her learning and interpersonal style.

Meeting Logistics: Have Her Sit Across from You

Women interpret eye contact differently than men. When someone is not looking them in the eye, the female brain processes this as a red flag that may indicate danger. Therefore, consistent eye contact with your female client is important. An easy way to make sure you have consistent eye contact with the female client is to have the woman sit directly across from you during the meeting. This positioning will help to engender trust and allow you to regularly make eye contact without a lot of effort.

At the second annual conference of the Financial Therapy Association in 2010, the opening keynote speaker Olivia Mellan, money coach and author of several books including *The Client Connection: How Advisors Can Build Bridges That Last*, stated that this practical technique is based on gender research. She also shared that male clients are most comfortable sitting beside the advisor and looking at the reports on a screen in front of them. This seating arrangement minimizes competitiveness and facilitates a more collaborative spirit.[3]

By simply altering your sitting arrangement, you can be more effective when coaching and advising couples.

Meeting Management: Make Sure She Tells Her Story

Women connect and build relationships by sharing details of their life verbally. Make sure that your female client has an ample opportunity to share her story during every couples meeting. Practice active listening, and reflect back what you heard her say. Allow her an opportunity to clarify her point and to ask any questions she may have. Remember the female brain loves details, so she may need more information than her male partner to make a financial decision. Allow her this space and time in each meeting.

What happens if her husband won't let you get a word in? Simply ask her the same questions you ask him and set limits with him. Do this politely by asking him to be quiet for a minute as you want to hear her perspective. Reassure him he will get an opportunity to give his opinion when she is done talking. And then make sure you honor this commitment.

Modeling to couples how to have a healthy money conversation starts with showing them that it is vital for each individual to speak and be heard. Redirecting the conversation to her, if she is the less-dominant communicator, is not only an important female-friendly strategy, it is a good teaching tool.

IN HER OWN WORDS

Grant my husband some patience! My advisor periodically starts off explaining whatever we're discussing in a manner I understand and then my husband, Mr. Finance Major, takes over. It's like my husband has to prove to the advisor he knows what's going on and it causes me to shut down.

—*KARA LYNN, 54-YEAR-OLD MARRIED CORPORATE EXECUTIVE*

Communication: Use Analogies and Stories She Can Relate To

Find out what interests your female clients and then incorporate some analogies or stories into your meetings that resonate with her. Does she like to read, knit, play tennis, watch hockey, or listen to music? Whatever her interests, using storytelling and examples framed around these hobbies is a great way to make her feel included and appreciated. Make sure you don't completely ditch what was working for him; simply be aware of what might work for her, too.

Also make sure you lose the jargon. Female clients (and male clients, too) often stop listening when you start talking in financial lingo and acronyms. Keep all your communication as simple and direct as possible. All professions have industry-specific language as a shorthand for communication. Make sure you only use jargon with your colleagues and "client speak" with your clients.

Trust Building: Meet with Her Individually

Women are socialized to put other people's needs first and their needs second. This happens in all areas of life, including in advising meetings with their partners. To make sure you understand her financial goals and objectives, it is a good idea to meet with her individually at the beginning of the couple's engagement. This meeting is a great way to help her identify and clarify her values, goals, and

---

IN HER OWN WORDS

My eyes glaze over when I think of my financial advisor. He is too technical. My husband and I both have trouble following him. Last meeting, I asked him to explain it in more simple terms and he got offended. The only reason I stay is it is too much work to find somebody new.

—SUZANNE, *43-YEAR-OLD MARRIED ENTREPRENEUR*

financial objectives. This may be the first time she has considered her financial needs separate from her family's and is a great way to start building a foundation of trust with her. You can answer any questions she might have about working with you and allow you to express the importance of her input in the couple's financial plan. As you learned in Chapter 7, "Fostering Financial Confidence," this meeting also helps her boost her financial self-esteem.

Performance Review: Tie Results to Real-Life Goals and Objectives

When you are communicating performance results to couples, make sure you balance his needs with hers. Most women prefer to hear performance results relative to real-life goals and objectives. In your annual meetings, make sure you share the couple's portfolio gains and/or losses relative to how this impacts goals such as saving for the kids' college, paying for vacations, or funding charitable interests. You can still report results relative to standard financial benchmarks, but know that this may work well for the male client but leave the female client flat. While women can be just as competitive as men, they view wealth differently and more often than not, see money as a way to secure their children's future or fund their dreams.

Summary

Advising couples is a challenging and rewarding part of being an advisor. More art than science, it requires that you are a consistent advocate for the couple as a whole. The only way to do this is to make sure the woman's voice is included in the dialogue too. Take the time to get to know her and how she prefers to work with you. Make sure you balance your time and attention between her and her partner, and most of all, let her know she is an important part of the couple's financial team.

Your Next Step: Advising Women in Couples Inventory

Select an upcoming meeting to test your skills in advising couples. The first time you do this assessment, you may want to pick a couple you have worked with for a while and who are fairly easy to advise. Prior to the meeting, read through the inventory questions below so that these items are top of mind in your appointment. During the meeting, periodically check in with yourself and notice your natural tendencies relative to eye contact, body language, questioning, and facilitating the conversation. Immediately following the meeting, before you do any other tasks, take five minutes to fill out the Advising Women in Couples Inventory below.

On a scale from "1" to "5," rate your performance relative to each of the following statements:

1	2	3	4	5
Strongly Disagree	Disagree	Neutral	Agree	Strongly Agree

1. I made eye contact with both members of the couple throughout the meeting.
2. I used open body language to show my interest in what both members were saying.
3. I asked my female client directly, clarifying questions, even if her partner already answered them.
4. I made a point of asking my female client about the family and what was going on in her life in general.
5. I listened more than I spoke.
6. I "balanced the triangle" throughout the appointment.
7. I balanced my communication style to balance gender differences in the meeting (i.e., using headlines versus details, stories and analogies that each could relate to, etc.).

8.   I walked away with a clear understanding of what the couple needs as well as what my female client needs from me during the next quarter.

How did you do? If you scored mostly 4s and 5s, congratulations, you are skilled at including her in the couples meeting. If you scored lower in some areas, make a commitment to improve these skills in the coming months. With practice, they will become second nature.

If you would like to take this coaching exercise to the next level, have a trusted colleague or assistant sit in on your next couples meeting to observe your interpersonal style. After the meeting, fill out the inventory and have the observer complete one as well. Next, discuss the scores, noting any discrepancies between what the observer noticed and your own ratings. Often it takes someone who is not actively involved in the meeting to point out areas to work on. After three months of practice, have the observer join you again and redo the exercise. Where did you improve most? Where might you be stuck? Make a plan to address the areas that need a little more development.

9

Preparing the Next Generation to Receive Wealth

*The father buys, the son builds, the grandchild sells,
and his son begs.*

—Scottish proverb

IN AN EPISODE OF THE AWARD-WINNING TELEVISION SHOW *30 ROCK*, Jack Donahy, Liz Lemon's boss, a wealthy corporate executive played by the actor Alec Baldwin, declares, "The first generation works their fingers to the bone making things, the next generation goes to college and innovates new ideas, and the third generation . . . snowboards and takes improv classes." Translated, Jack Donahy means that the first generation creates wealth, the second generation enjoys an affluent lifestyle, and the third generation spends all the money. This example shows that the concept of affluent families failing to sustain wealth across generations is showing up in pop culture, which speaks volumes about the scope and seriousness of this problem.

Why does this happen to so many wealthy families? Because many wealth creators are new to their affluence, did not have parents who taught them the skills and knowledge to make their wealth last for future generations, and therefore, are navigating the land of wealth without a road map. Historically, this passing of wealth was viewed as a man's job. However, with the increase in women controlling and creating wealth, this is changing. Your affluent female client is an important part of the intergenerational wealth puzzle. Therefore, she needs a caring financial advisor like you to guide her and her family on how to best transfer wealth and prepare the next generation to receive it. Not only does this help her successfully transfer assets, it is an opportunity to pass on family values, continue the family's legacy, and for you to meet the next generation.

Reality Check

In the book *Preparing Heirs: Five Steps to a Successful Transition of Family Wealth and Values*, the authors Roy Williams and Vic Preisser reveal that 70 percent of families fail to successfully pass down wealth to future generations and only 3 percent miscarry due to technical errors.[1] The difference between the families that succeed in passing down wealth versus those that do not are they practice open communication about money, have an ability to resolve family conflicts, and take a proactive approach to preparing the next generation to receive the wealth. Next generation preparation includes financial literacy training, understanding and appreciating family values, and knowing how to emotionally handle the responsibilities that come from inheriting family wealth.

As this client need is more recognized by the financial services industry, many firms are adding intergenerational wealth services to their offerings. These services include assisting with the financial aspects of estate planning and passing on wealth through trusts and other financial vehicles, facilitating family wealth conversations and meetings, preparing heirs to financially and emotionally receive wealth, legacy planning, and family governance. While many in the industry consider these offerings as only appropriate for ultra-high-net-worth families, these services are much needed by clients in the high-net-worth category as well. In addition, women play a vital role in this process, making it a very female-friendly offering. These services have been shown to increase client trust and client satisfaction ratings and assist advisors in retaining assets across generations.

Desire Does Not Equal Action

In 2005, the Allianz Life American Legacies Study was conducted. In this study, researchers asked high-net-worth individuals how comfortable they were at having wealth transfer conversations with the next generation. Seventy-one percent of the traditional generation and 68 percent of the baby boomers reported being confident having these conversations with their adult children. However, when researchers went one step further and asked if they were actually engaging in these dialogues, they discovered that only 31 percent of traditionalists and 29 percent of baby boomers were actually talking to the next generation about money.[2]

This study highlights how desire does not always translate into action. In a society where money and wealth is still a relatively taboo topic, it is challenging for your affluent female clients to speak up and initiate these conversations. Chances are they grew up with parents who did not discuss family wealth openly, either because they did not have money or they believed it was rude and inappropriate to discuss with the children. The result is many of your clients need you to initiate the conversation. When you do, these clients are often grateful and open to engaging in this process with their children. Their hope, like most parents, is to give their children what they did not have—preparation and training to receive and live with wealth.

As with any type of estate or wealth transfer planning, talking about what will happen after your death tends to make clients (and some advisors) anxious. Intellectually, your female clients may know this is a valuable service, but they may find themselves, like so many others, fearful of what these conversations will stir up in them and their families. This reluctance to openly address the human side of an intergenerational transfer results in many affluent women and their families avoiding these conversations because they can be uncomfortable. Ultimately, these same women and their families lose the family wealth within a generation or two of its creation. As their advisor, you need to identify these emotional roadblocks, coach them on how to overcome these obstacles, and then help the next generation do the same.

Common Roadblocks

Let's take a look at the common fears that women face when considering intergenerational wealth services. As you read through each one, notice if you also face this fear when working with your clients around this topic.

Fear of Talking About Money

While modern day parents discuss sex, drugs, and safe Internet practices, they stop short of talking about money and wealth. The reason is because discussing money openly in our society has long been a taboo subject. Seen as showy, bragging, or just plain rude, these conversations are to be avoided and often result in heirs receiving sizeable trusts with little preparation or warning. The family silence about money and inheritance is often intended to "help" the children live a normal life; however, this strategy backfires as it produces young adults who are very ill-prepared to handle wealth in a responsible way.

The taboo around talking about money is starting to shift, especially among affluent women. According to a *Women and Affluence Survey*, conducted by Women & Co. in 2010, wealthy women are more likely to openly discuss money in the wake of the 2008 recession. The report found that 91 percent of women are discussing money with their family members and 65 percent think that money talk is not nearly as frowned upon as it was prerecession.[3] Not only are these women talking more about money with family members, they are making a point to discuss money matters with their daughters. As money becomes a more acceptable topic of conversation, your job of initiating money dialogues with clients around intergenerational wealth transfers should become easier.

Fear of Losing Financial Control

Many older clients, including women, worry that as they age, their children will take control over their finances. This fear of loss of control is a normal part of human development and needs to be recognized and appreciated by you, the advisor. Address these concerns head on by letting your client know that the purpose of an intergenerational wealth conversation is not to take control away,

---

IN HER OWN WORDS

My dad was a big part of the reason why we did not "talk about those things." For years my older brother had been trying to get my dad to write down his financial information, to no avail. When I finished writing my book, I asked my dad to sit with me and go through it. He agreed, but when we got to the finances he said, "I don't want you to know my bank account numbers!" I explained to him that I didn't want to know them, but it would be so helpful to know that they are written down, and if anything did happen I would know where to find them. He thought that was a good plan. We spent two days together gathering names of his attorneys and financial planners, talking about his estate plan, his funeral, and the charities to which he wanted to contribute to upon his death. I learned so much about my dad during those two days. It was very, very special.

—GWEN MORGAN, AUTHOR OF THE WHAT IF WORKBOOK

but to gain important feedback from her family so she can maintain oversight as long as she wishes. It is also an opportunity to work to communicate her family values to the next generation and to make sure her wishes are followed when she is no longer capable of managing her financial affairs.

Fear of Mortality

Another emotion that is triggered when considering intergenerational wealth conversations is the fear of dying. Most of us would rather be on the golf course playing the back nine than in an office discussing our inevitable death—even if we don't play golf!

The reality is that these conversations include talking about how your client wants to be cared for if she becomes ill and how she wants to die. These end-of-life wishes naturally bring up a client's fear of mortality. It is important that you recognize these emotions as normal and explain to your client the importance of having these

---

IN HER OWN WORDS

When my Aunt Jeanette passed away in 2000, my cousin Michelle was so calm and collected at the funeral. I asked her how she was so relaxed and she told me her mom had written everything down beforehand . . . the dress she wanted to be laid out in, that she wanted her bible and rosary buried with her, that her mom and dad had already purchased their burial plot and had the headstone engraved with their names and birthdates, that she had been given a list of the family finances, where the important documents were, etc. I thought to myself, "What a gift from a parent to a child . . . to take the time to put their affairs in order before a crisis happens, while the parent is still of sound mind and body and able to make good decisions."

—*SHEVAUN, 41 YEARS OLD, MARRIED, MOTHER OF TWO*

dialogues now when she is healthy enough to do so. Too many families have not had the benefit of knowing what their parents wanted and were left to make these difficult decisions at very emotional times.

There are workbooks and tools that you can use to help guide this discussion with your clients. A few are listed in the Female-Friendly Resource Guide at the back of this book. This type of structure helps clients stay on track in these sometimes emotional conversations and also provides you with some guidance on how to proceed. One of the great benefits of having a dialogue about end-of-life wishes and about the human side of estate planning is that it can be a very rewarding experience. For some, it increases intimacy in the here and now. For others, it simply takes a future difficult time in their life a little easier.

Fear of Failing as a Parent

Another fear that your client may face is the one that she has not been a good enough parent. Women are especially vulnerable to second-guessing their parenting decisions. Should she have stayed home with the kids instead of working 60-hour weeks at the law firm? Should she have insisted her husband be home more regularly for family dinner? Should she have been calmer, stricter, and so on, with the children? The list of potential questions goes on. Just know that many female clients have mixed feelings about how well they raised their children and may bump up against these feelings when doing intergenerational wealth planning.

Reassure your female client that there is no such thing as a "perfect parent," and you are not sitting in judgment of her skills in this area. Sharing with your client the fact that you are not a perfect parent yourself or that you know many families struggling with similar concerns can really help alleviate this anxiety. In addition, assure her that in your role as the facilitator you will make sure the conversation stays on track and does not deteriorate into mommy bashing. Often the children are actually thankful for the opportunity to have this conversation with their parent(s), and this fear is unfounded. However, if the family is not able to engage in a healthy conversation without fighting about past hurts, it indicates that a referral to a family therapist or a family wealth consultant skilled in helping families resolve conflicts is warranted.

Fear of Looking Incompetent

Another common roadblock is the fear of looking incompetent. Let's face it, no one likes to appear foolish or uncertain. Often your affluent female clients are polished professionals who were raised to keep up appearances. Talking to spouses, loved ones, and children about money and wealth may tap into her fear of not appearing self-assured and confident. While it is okay and may even be preferable for her not to have all the answers in this dialogue, it is a new role that may take some time getting used to. Interestingly enough, this is also the biggest fear advisors face in offering these services because it requires you to take off your "expert" hat and instead facilitate an often messy and uncertain process.

The best way to address this concern is to remind your female client that there is no perfect way to have a family financial conversation or to pass on wealth. Most clients feel anxiety when approaching this work, but the majority of them also find great solace after doing so. Assure her that you will figure it out together and it is okay to not have all the answers. Whether an immigrant or a native to the land of wealth, chances are she is cutting a new trail when she is approaching this topic with her family.

Now that you know more about the common fears that block clients from initiating and having intergenerational wealth conversations, it is time to take a look at how generational differences may play a role in these meetings.

Working Across Generations

Part of what makes intergenerational wealth conversations and transfers challenging and interesting is they involve family members from multiple generations. Each generation has its shared historical, social, and life experiences that impact how members of a particular generation think, act, and communicate. These differences can thwart the process, unless you appreciate and factor in these various viewpoints into your work with your female client and her family.

Take a minute and answer the following question. If you are going out to dinner tonight, how will you decide where to eat? Chances are if you were born before 1945, making you a member of the traditionalist generation, you will go to the restaurant on the corner that you have been going to for the past 30 years. If you were born after 1980, you are a member of the millennial generation, sometimes called generation Y. You probably will send out a tweet on Twitter to your followers or post an update on Facebook to your friends, asking for restaurant recommendations. If you are born in between the traditionalist and generation Y, you are either a baby boomer or generation Xer and likely to surf the Internet for restaurant ideas and then call a friend on the phone to discuss your options.

There is no right or wrong way to find a restaurant. However, these different avenues point to how the generation you belong to impacts your view of the world, communication preferences, and interpersonal style. When working across multiple generations, it is important to understand these factors. Let's look briefly at each generation and its primary characteristics below.

Traditionalists (Born Before 1945)

Traditionalists grew up under the shadow of the Great Depression and, during their early lifetime, witnessed two World Wars. They grew up knowing how to live and do without and, therefore, can be quite frugal. In general, people from this generation have strong beliefs when it comes to patriotism, hard work, and respect for leaders. Traditionalists were influenced by such people as Joe McCarthy, Dr. Spock, and President Franklin Delano Roosevelt. Growing up, they got their news from coffee shops, from church, from socializing at the kitchen table with neighbors, and/or by turning on the radio. People from this generation can best be described by the word *loyal*.

Interestingly enough, about 50 percent of traditionalist men served in the armed forces, so there is a tendency to take a top-down approach when getting things done.[4] This may be a challenge in an intergenerational family financial meeting since it conflicts with others' views of how decisions should be made, especially those clients from generation Y who like to have a say in everything!

Baby Boomers (1946–1964)

Baby boomers were raised by parents who convinced them that they could make the world a better place. This created idealism among this generation as evidenced by the influential people and events of this time period, including Martin Luther King, Jr., and the civil rights movement, President John F. Kennedy and the NASA Space Program, and Gloria Steinem and the women's rights movement. Boomers went to Woodstock, preached peace and free love, and fought against the Vietnam War. They were the first generation to have television sets in their homes and the first to witness the consumer goods industry explode. Boomers bought things a traditionalist would never consider—like a pet rock or a mood ring; and they used television sets for news and to entertain friends and family.

Boomers can best be described by the word *optimistic*. This optimism resulted from this generation having availability to just about everything, from food to consumer goods to jobs and education. It also helped them create wealth through innovation and new ideas. As you might imagine, this idealism many times conflicts with traditionalist views of loyalty and frugality.

Generation X (Born between 1965–1979)

Sometimes called the "me generation," generation X grew up in a time of financial, family, and societal insecurity. People from this generation witnessed businesses merging and downsizing. As a result, they tend to focus on getting their own needs met versus being loyal to "the company," such as what a traditionalist would do. Known for their independent and entrepreneurial spirits, generation Xers experienced rapid changes such as the AIDS epidemic, the introduction of MTV, and an increase in worldwide competition due to globalization. There were many scandals during this time period, including the O. J. Simpson murder trial, President Clinton's inappropriate relationship with Monica Lewinsky, and the Enron scandal. For the first time, news was available 24 hours a day, 7 days a week. This fierce competition led to ratings being fueled by the first media outlet to expose a fallen hero or a corrupt institution. VCRs morphed into DVDs and fax machines were replaced by e-mail. Online social networking became a substitute for the baby boomers' networking dinners. All these changes led generation Xers to be best described by the word *skepticism*. This perspective came from the world and the people in it changing so rapidly around them, but not necessarily for the greater good.

In family wealth conversations, generation X members may be skeptical about advisors from larger firms. They may be more independent than baby boomers or individuals from generation Y as they grew up living in a time where company loyalty no longer existed and the optimism of the boomer era had died. It may take more time to earn their trust and to assure them that you are looking out for their parents and their best interests.

Millennials/Generation Y (Born between 1980–2000)

This is a generation characterized as smart, practical, and techno savvy. Millennials, also referred to as generation Y, is the most educated generation. It is a generation that knows no world without computers or, for most members, without the Internet. Being bombarded with technology and media has resulted in a blurred line between what is real and what is not in their world. The message this generation received growing up with baby boomer parents is "you can be anything you want to be" and "you are a winner." Millennials grew up given choices about nearly everything—what kind of drink to have with dinner, where the next family vacation would take place, and what kind of computer they wanted for their birthday. They are used to immediate gratification, with texting and social media being their primary mode of connection and communication.

The result is that this generation is used to being catered to and believes all decisions should be collaborative. Members of this generation don't like to be told what to do by authority figures, so you can imagine how this conflicts with the views of the traditionalists. The word that best characterizes this generation is *choice*.

The need for millennials to have a say in everything may trigger fear of loss of control in the elders in the family. Remember, to communicate with this generation you need to think about how texting and social media can be used in the process. Millennials live online, so if you plan on engaging them in intergenerational wealth conversations and services, you need to be technologically savvy to earn their respect.

For those children born after 2002, the jury is still out as to how they will be impacted by the events of their time. There is yet to be an official name for this generation; however, experts agree that the failure of the financial markets in 2008 and the resulting recession is likely to impact them greatly. This generation is already more frugal and socially responsible than the one before it. Some say that the values of the traditionalist generation may be reinstituted as individuals discover the risk involved in overuse of credit and home equity to fund purchases. One thing is sure: this generation will continue to rely heavily on technology to interact, connect, and communicate with the world around them.

Understanding and appreciating generational differences will help you communicate, facilitate, and approach intergenerational wealth conversations in a prudent manner. There is no right viewpoint on how to connect, but showing an appreciation for others' preferences is an important step to bridging generational gaps and helping members from multiple generations come together to talk about and plan for the future.

Why You?

Now that you know more about the complexities of talking with your female clients and their families about wealth and how to factor in generational differences, you may be wondering, "Why me?" My answer is "Why not you?" The business of money is an emotional one. The best financial advisors not only develop concrete financial plans and investment strategies, they also coach their clients to undercover thoughts, beliefs, and feelings about money. Not only is this type of exploration a good fit for many female clients, it is something that helps the family preserve and pass on wealth.

Your financial expertise, good communication skills, and access to clients willing to talk about money provide the perfect setting for intergenerational wealth services. While some would consider these conversations more in the realm of a family counselor or psychotherapist, most mental health professionals are ill-prepared and often unwilling to delve into their client's relationship with money. While organizations such as The Financial Therapy Association are working to train more mental health professionals in this area, they do not have the financial expertise and access to clients that you do.

Affluent women and their families are busy; therefore, addressing family communication skills and financial literacy training in your office is not only prudent, it is convenient. Most of what needs to be taught and practiced is very doable, and often advisors who do this type of coaching find it very rewarding.

How to Introduce Intergenerational Wealth Services

As you know, female clients like to feel understood, and they appreciate it when you inquire about important people in their lives. Therefore, by listening carefully and asking some open-ended questions, you can improve your relationship with your client and also pinpoint any potential need for intergenerational wealth services.

One of the best ways to introduce these services is to simply listen for life events in your client's life. These life events can be positive, such as births, graduations, weddings, and anniversaries, or negative, such as deaths, divorces, and illness. Both represent an opportunity for you to ask questions about your client's plans regarding her wealth. Using positive life events to spur an intergenerational wealth dialogue is preferable because your client is less burdened by grief and loss and more able to engage in the conversation.

The next time you meet with her and her partner, ask about the family. What has changed in the family? Does she have any concerns about her children or parents? If her daughter is looking at colleges, discuss how it may be a good time for her to share how she paid for college and her wishes for her daughter's education. If her son is having his first baby, maybe it is a good time to start exploring what family legacy she would like to pass on to her new grandchild. Whatever is going on in her family, get curious, ask questions, and look for ways to tie this back to how you can help her with intergenerational wealth services.

In addition to asking questions, listen for subtext in your client's comments. Does she complain about her stepdaughter overspending? Or does she reference her mother's frailty? These are great times to ask open-ended questions to uncover what is going on in your client's life and how you might work with her to plan for her financial future. Issues that concern family also give you clues and an opening to educate her about intergenerational wealth services and how you can help her successfully pass down her wealth.

Lastly, educate your clients on the dangers of not proactively preparing their children to receive wealth. Your female clients may not be aware of the high rate of failure when it comes to sustaining family wealth across generations. By letting them know about these risks and the steps they can take to minimize them in their families, you have strengthened your advisor-client connection while providing them with a very valuable service.

How to Facilitate Intergenerational Wealth Conversations

Now that you have introduced her to intergenerational wealth services, it is time to look at how best to facilitate these conversations. Start by working with your client to identify her values, goals, and wishes. This is done through asking open-ended questions and exploring the four key areas, as shown in Figure 9.1, in intergenerational wealth planning.

Figure 9.1

Key Areas for Intergenerational Wealth Planning

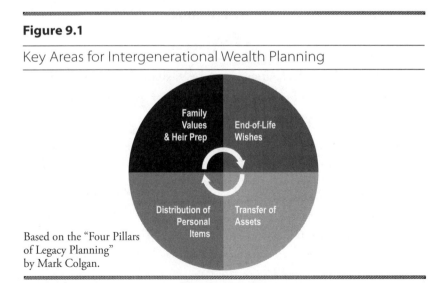

Family Values & Heir Prep

End-of-Life Wishes

Distribution of Personal Items

Transfer of Assets

Based on the "Four Pillars of Legacy Planning" by Mark Colgan.

These include plans for the transfer of real estate and financial assets, distribution of assets with little or no financial value but high personal value, communication of end-of-life instructions and wishes, and sharing of the family history, values, and intended legacy.[5] You are probably comfortable discussing the transfer of real estate and financial assets, but may be less skilled or familiar with talking about the other three areas.

Below are a few questions you can ask in each of these areas to get the dialogue started:

Distribution of Assets of Emotional Value

1. What family heirlooms do you have and how do you plan on passing them down to the next generation?
2. Is there a story that goes with this particular item, and do your children or grandchildren know it?
3. What makes passing this item down to this person(s) important to you? How might you communicate this to the receiver of this possession?

End-of-Life Instructions and Wishes

4. Do you have an updated durable power of attorney and living will? If so, have these documents been shared with your children and/or your assigned agents? Why or why not?
5. Do you have any special wishes for how you will be cared for if you become ill? If so, are these in writing and have they been communicated to your children or related parties?
6. What else would you want a caregiver to know if you were unable to communicate these wishes directly to this person? What steps might you take to make sure your wishes are clear?

Family History, Values, and Legacy

1. What do your children and grandchildren know about how the family wealth was created? What lessons do you want them to take from this success story and pass down to their children?

2. How did your parents prepare you financially to receive wealth, and what would you like to do in the same way with your children and/or grandchildren? What would you like to do differently?

3. What family legacy would you like to leave behind, and what makes this legacy important to you?

These questions are only a guide for you to begin the discussion. There are many more questions and avenues to explore. Let your client guide you on where she wants to go and remember that some areas may be more difficult for her to discuss than others. Give her as much time as she needs to talk about her wealth, her intentions for passing it on to her family, and/or her charitable causes. She may want to have these conversations alone or with her partner in the room. Either way, she will gain clarity in time and be ready to invite others in for a family meeting. Before doing so, review these tips for facilitating intergenerational wealth conversations with her and work to develop a plan that you are both comfortable with.

◆ **Tip 1: Identify a specific goal for the meeting.** Before your client meets with her family, help her identify one or two specific goals for the conversation. She may want to share her success story as a way to communicate her values to the next generation or ask for input from her partner or parents about how best to foster financial responsibility in the next generation. Whatever her intended goal, make sure it is small and doable.

Consider role-playing with her to identify any difficulties she might have in communicating her feelings about these goals. Brainstorm how to cope with the different personalities in the room and any anticipated problems that might arise. Keep in mind that clients often have more anxiety anticipating the meeting than when they are actually engaged in it. This is a normal response since most clients have not openly talked about these topics with family members before. Assure her that with practice and patience these conversations will get easier.

At the start of the appointment, communicate the agreed-upon goals to help everyone stay on track. When and if you find the dialogue has veered off course, then gently remind the group of the original goals.

♦ **Tip 2: Agree to disagree.** The goal of a family meeting is not to get everyone to agree with your client's viewpoint. Instead it is to open the lines of communication, to hear different perspectives, and to foster understanding across generations. Encourage your client and her family members to agree to disagree at the beginning of the meeting. This allows everyone to be less defensive and, for you as the facilitator, to remind the group of this agreement should unproductive conflict arise.

♦ **Tip 3: Use "I" statements.** As with all effective listening, encourage your client and those in attendance to share with the group using "I" statements. Using "I" statements helps participants not to point blame toward others but to speak only about their experience. Refer back to Chapter 6, "Active Listening," to refresh your memory on the tenets of listening.

♦ **Tip 4: Be respectful.** Talking about money and wealth can get emotional. Money is often tied to deeper psychological concerns such as love, acceptance, self-worth, safety, and security. While the goal of a family meeting is not to dig up past hurts, tensions may arise. Therefore, it is always important that all members in the meeting treat each other with respect. This is done by listening actively to each other, not interrupting, and refraining from using profanity or blaming language. If the family is unable to consistently follow these guidelines, it may be a sign that they need to be referred to a specialist, such as a family wealth consultant who will teach families how to resolve conflicts and communicate more effectively. How to make a referral to one of these specialists is covered later in this chapter.

◆ **Tip 5: Encourage curiosity.** Curiosity is a great tool for increasing understanding and facilitating a healthy dialogue. Encourage your female client and her meeting attendees to let go of defending their positions and instead to get curious about their loved one's thoughts. When you are busy wondering about where the other person is coming from, you learn more and your mind is too preoccupied to pick a fight. Therefore, encourage everyone in the meeting to wonder more and fight less.

There are many other strategies and tools to use when conducting a family meeting and helping female clients engage in intergenerational wealth conversations. However, the practical and easy-to-implement tools presented here should get you started off in the right direction. Facilitating an intergenerational wealth conversation is not a onetime event, but an ongoing process. As situations change and life events arise, clients may need to revisit or work through new concerns.

One of the key areas included in any intergenerational wealth discussion is how to prepare the heirs to receive wealth. Let's look at some ways you can engage your client and her family in this important part of the process.

Raising Financially Responsible Children

The second part of helping female clients pass down wealth to the next generation is to assist them in raising financially responsible children. According to the 2011 World Wealth Report by Merrill Lynch, 69 percent of high-net-worth individuals surveyed agree that the next generation is not adequately prepared to manage their inheritance.[6] While this is unsettling, it is a place where you can add value for your female clients and make a real difference in their lives.

It is not surprising that one of the greatest fears an affluent mother has is raising a child who is ill-equipped to manage the demands and responsibilities of wealth. No parent, no matter what their economic status, wants to see a child become entitled and waste his or her life away partying into the wee hours of the night. This fear is often combated by not talking about money and wealth with the hopes that her child will escape unharmed. However, the plethora of wealthy heir's sex tapes, drug convictions, stints in rehab, and general bad behavior depicted in the media indicates that not talking about it does not work. Instead your female clients need help addressing these concerns head-on with their children. They need your guidance and expertise to assist them in rearing well-balanced children who are financially literate and emotionally capable of inheriting wealth.

Most women are relieved to find out that these risks can be mitigated by practicing open family communication and teaching the next generation how to manage money properly. They are further comforted by the fact that you can help them with this task and that the best course of action is to involve multiple family members in the training program. They don't have to do this alone.

Raising financially thoughtful children involves more than just teaching young people about the mechanics of money. It also involves teaching them about money personalities and how to be emotionally intelligent when it comes to managing wealth.

Let's take a look at each of the components shown in Figure 9.2 in greater detail.

Figure 9.2

Preparing the Next Generation to Receive Wealth

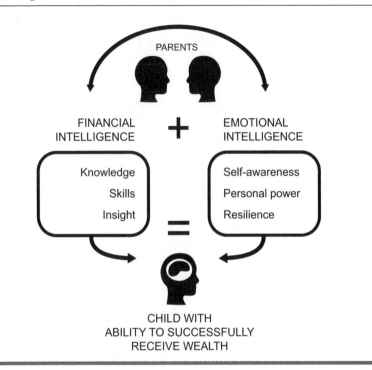

Financial Intelligence

Financial intelligence is defined as having the financial knowledge and skills, and the insight into your relationship with money so you can responsibly save, spend, invest, and pass on wealth. *Knowledge* includes understanding basic financial concepts, such as budgeting, saving, investing, and charitable giving. *Skills* refers to using this knowledge to perform basic financial tasks, such as balancing a checkbook, calculating compound interest, and reading and understanding financial documents. The last component, *financial insight*, is defined as having an understanding of the underlying thoughts, feelings, and attitudes that influence your financial behaviors. While some financial literacy programs leave out learning about money personalities and financial insight, this is actually a very important component to financial intelligence. It is only when a person can understand how they make financial decisions and the values they are expressing through these habits that they can learn how to live at peace with money and wealth.

A person's money personality is typically formed between the ages of 5 and 14. This is the time when children and young adolescents are witnessing parents, grandparents, and other important caregivers manage money. By watching others talk, save, spend, and invest money, the young person develops a set of beliefs, called *money scripts*. These money scripts follow the young person into adulthood and influence his or her financial habits. If a solid foundation is laid and a child understands how to identify money beliefs and attitudes in the decision-making process, unhealthy financial behaviors can be avoided later in life.

The best way to teach children about money is to start early and be consistent in your efforts. The learning and conversations you will have with a child need to be age appropriate. For instance, you would not talk about financial markets with a 5-year-old, but you may teach him the names of different coins and paper money as well as the monetary value of each. As the child grows and matures, the lessons taught change and advance in complexity. If your client has not taken the initiative to teach her children financial literacy skills

---

In Her Own Words

My parents were very good at fostering financial independence. If I wanted something, I had to work for it. I can remember a feeling of self-satisfaction the day I paid for my first car with $2,000 of hard-earned cash.

—LISA, 32 YEARS OLD, SINGLE INHERITOR AND BUSINESS OWNER

from an early age, do not worry. These lessons can be taught at any age, and it is never too late to begin.

A great resource for how to help your clients teach their children about money is the book written by Joline Godfrey titled *Raising Financially Fit Kids.*[7] This book uses childhood developmental theory and 10 basic money skills to guide parents on how to raise financially literate children. The 10 basic money skills include:

1. How to save
2. How to keep track of money
3. How to get paid what you are worth
4. How to spend wisely
5. How to talk about money
6. How to live on a budget
7. How to invest
8. How to exercise the entrepreneurial spirit
9. How to handle credit
10. How to use money to change the world

The book contains activities, discussion topics, and resources for further exploration of each of these money skills appropriate for different age groups. For instance, you can coach your female clients to help their young children, ages 5 to 8, spend money wisely by setting parameters for spending prior to going to the toy store. If the child knows he has $10 to spend in the store and he wants a toy that is $12, then encourage your client to discuss the difference between the cost of the item and his budget. Your client should help him evaluate his choices and enforce that the budget remains unchanged at $10. This activity teaches the child how to factor in his wants and needs compared to his budget. The part that most parents will need your help with will be sticking to the budget even when the child becomes upset. While it is hard for parents to watch their children cry, it is a vital financial lesson that you can't have everything you see. Eventually, the crying will stop and the foundation for sound spending will be set.

Now consider the same money lesson on how to spend money wisely, but for a 13- to 15-year-old. To work on this money skill at this age, coach your female client to discuss competitive pricing with her son. If he wants to buy a video game player, have him conduct a price comparison of three brands. Encourage him to use *Consumer Reports* and other information available on the Internet to make a selection. When he knows what he wants to purchase, have him present his analysis and discuss what he learned in the process.

Overall, coaching your clients to teach their children how to have a healthy relationship with money is a great value-added service. It draws on your existing expertise, and it shows your client that you care about the well-being of her entire family. It also helps you determine your client's current level of financial intelligence and identify and fill in any gaps in her basic money skills. With a little creativity, you and she can have fun, further solidify your advisor-client relationship, and help prepare the next generation to receive wealth.

Emotional Intelligence

In addition to learning financial intelligence, a young person needs to develop a high level of emotional intelligence to be able to skillfully navigate the land of wealth. *Emotional intelligence* is defined as having an ability to identify and express feelings and understand how your words and actions impact those around you. An heir with high emotional intelligence is less likely to be burdened by wealth, less likely to be ripped off by unethical business and financial associates, and more likely to live a satisfying life. He or she has self-awareness, a sense of personal power in the world, and the resilience to bounce back from life's challenges.

While inheriting wealth is seen by the outside world as a wonderful gift, it can be a complex and confusing life transition for the beneficiary. This is especially true if money was not openly discussed or was a constant source of family conflict. Common feelings associated with receiving wealth include grief, loss, depression, fear, guilt, joy, and relief. Because money is not openly discussed in our society, those who receive wealth are often left feeling confused by their ambivalence toward the money. Your role as an advisor is to coach your female clients on how to prepare their children to understand that inheriting money can be a mixed blessing. Let them know it is okay to feel many different things about the money and it is important to talk about these emotions. If not expressed verbally, often these feelings get acted out through the use of destructive behaviors.

As mentioned in Chapter 3, "Your Affluent Female Client," some individuals experience wealth as a weight, or emotional burden. It is not uncommon for these children to enter adulthood without finding out what they want to do with their lives. These individuals run the risk of using and abusing drugs and alcohol or developing eating disorders or shopping addictions to fill the void. These destructive behaviors can be avoided by helping clients teach their children a vocabulary to describe different emotional states and how to communicate and resolve conflict as a family. While this may be out of your area of expertise, you can be an important catalyst to encouraging this type of personal development. Offer your female clients books on raising emotionally intelligent children, resources on parenting affluent children, and a kind ear to listen to her triumphs and challenges in this area. (For more resources on the topic of financial and emotional intelligence, refer to the Female-Friendly Resource Guide at the back of this book.)

When to Hire a Consultant

In some instances, it makes sense for you to refer your female client and her family to a family wealth consultant, family therapist, or mental health professional. If the family is dealing with serious mental health issues, such as addictions, depression, eating disorders, trauma, and/or schizophrenia, a referral to a mental health professional is appropriate because you do not have the specialized training required to treat these illnesses. Also, if you meet with the family but find that they are unable to work through conflicts in your office and stay stuck on certain areas of contention, then a referral to a family therapist or family wealth consultant is probably prudent. Lastly, if you find yourself working with a family that has a complicated structure, such as multiple stepchildren and grandchildren, a special-needs child, or a complex wealth picture, consider bringing in a family wealth consultant to work alongside you. Often, having two specialists in the meetings with different, but complementary, skills is the best way to proceed.

When making a referral, be candid about your concerns and why you feel that another type of professional would be better qualified to help. Do not diagnose or label the person or the family, but instead simply state the behavior or set of behaviors that is concerning to you. Remind your client throughout the referral process that you care and want her and her family to have the best chance of success and that sometimes the best way to help a client is to refer her and her family to a specialist. Reassure the client that this does not mean you are abandoning her (unless it does mean you are terminating the relationship), but that you are simply adding another member to her financial team who is better-equipped for her particular family situation.

Overall, clients are very receptive to referrals when you are comfortable and confident making them. If your client does not follow up with the referral, then it is up to you to decide how critical this step is to your work with her and her family. Keep in mind that often referrals to specialists are made several times before a client acts on the information.

Summary

Affluent female clients want your help with talking to family members about passing on wealth and with raising financially thoughtful children. By offering assistance in exploring the human side of intergenerational wealth transfers, you are providing a service that will improve your advisor-client relationship and position you as a trusted advisor for her and the entire family. While initially, holding family meetings and preparing the next generation to receive wealth may feel outside your comfort zone, with a little preparation, training, and practice, it could turn into one of the most rewarding parts of your practice.

Your Next Step: Adding Intergenerational Wealth Services into Your Practice

Now that you know the importance of having intergenerational wealth conversations and preparing the next generation to receive wealth, it is time to figure out how to incorporate these services into your practice. Below are five practical steps for taking what you have learned in this chapter and incorporating it into your practice.

Step 1. Analyze the benefits versus the risks. There are many long-term benefits to adding intergenerational wealth services into your business model, including asset retention, increased client satisfaction, market differentiation, and a greater number of high-quality word-of-mouth referrals. In addition, these types of family-oriented services tend to resonate with your affluent female client's desire to care for her family now and in the future. Before you do implement these services into your practice you also need to consider the short-term risks.[8] Take some time over the next week and answer the following questions:

- What is the long-term financial and nonfinancial benefit to adding this service to my practice?
- What is the best time to invest my time, talent, and financial resources into this offering?
- Are my margins strong enough to support this in the short run? In the long run?

If it makes good business sense to proceed at this time, go to step 2. If not, consider affiliating with a wealth psychology consultant or firm that specializes in intergenerational wealth consultation. By doing so, you will provide an important service to your affluent female clients without taking the business risk before you are ready.

Step 2. Target a few ideal female clients for these services. Once you have decided to move forward, identify one or two female clients who may be receptive to these services. Consider women you have been working with for a while and with whom you have established a firm foundation of trust. Select women who have relatively low conflict in their family. The healthier the family is, the higher likelihood of your being able to coach them successfully. In time, you can move on to more complex families and/or work with a family wealth consultant in these situations.

Step 3. Introduce the topic at your next meeting with targeted clients. Now that you have selected a client or two to start with, develop a plan for raising this topic at your next regularly scheduled meeting. There are several ways to start this conversation. In your client meetings, you can listen for life events that lend themselves to this type of discussion, such as births, deaths, graduations, and anniversaries. You can educate your client and her partner about the high percentage of families that fail to pass on wealth, and ask if she has any concerns in that area. Or you can review the parts of a sound intergenerational wealth plan—such as passing on family values and lessons, communicating end-of-life wishes, distributing personal possessions of emotional value, and finally transferring financial assets—and find out what areas may still need attention.

Step 4. Follow up with clients who are interested. Working on intergenerational wealth conversations and plans is not a onetime event. Set up a series of meetings with a female client who is interested, and develop a plan together based on her priorities, wishes, and needs. Include the next generations in the later meetings because it is important not only to devise a plan, but to communicate it to her future heirs. When in doubt on how to proceed, consult with a family wealth expert who can guide you and your client on the many facets of passing on wealth.

Step 5. Keep the dialogue alive. Make a commitment to keep the dialogue alive with clients who are interested in this service as well as with clients who have yet to sign up. Check in regularly with all your clients about intergenerational concerns. Write client newsletters on the topic, and offer client appreciation events that include guest speakers with expertise in this area.

Marketing to
Affluent Women

*Take the attitude of a student, never be too big
to ask questions, never know too much
to learn something new.*

—Og Mandino, bestselling author, *The Greatest Salesman in the World*

NOW THAT YOU KNOW HOW TO CONNECT, COMMUNICATE, AND collaborate with affluent female clients, both individually as well as when they are a member of a couple, it is time to think about developing a female-friendly marketing strategy. Of course, the best way to market your practice is through providing high-quality services and practicing the essential skills for advising affluent women detailed in this book. Simply by being a wonderful financial advisor for women of wealth, your practice will grow. However, any good business will have a marketing strategy to increase awareness of the company, its brand, and how a person or family can benefit from hiring the firm. In marketing to affluent women, it is vital that you have a keen understanding of the female brain, women's psychology, and common female financial concerns. You must then take this knowledge and transfer it into marketing messages that resonate with your ideal female client. For an industry that has catered to male wealth creators for so long, it requires revisiting some basic tenets of marketing and also incorporating what is known about how women buy and make hiring decisions relative to financial services.

Pink Is Not a Marketing Strategy

In 2012, Lego, the famous toy company, spent a lot of money developing a product line just for girls. They called this line Lego Friends and made it pink and purple and offered play sets, including a cafe, a beauty salon, and a bakery. This line was developed based on sound gender research, but when it hit the market, mothers were not happy.[1] Why couldn't their daughters play with the same Legos that their sons did that were red, blue, and green? Why did girls have to build with gender-specific Legos? Why couldn't they build whatever their little minds could dream of? The Lego company was publicly chastised for not empowering young girls. The company's intent was sound, but the execution of this idea was poor.

Another example of women's marketing gone wrong occurred in the late 1990s when the ski industry decided to first make women's equipment. However, instead of doing market research and creating a well-thought-out strategy for reaching out to female skiers, they got lazy and really only changed the color of their products. All of a sudden, every ski shop had a pair or two of ugly fuchsia (If you are color blind or male, read "really bright pink"!) ski boots. The boots were made for beginner skiers and other than being pink were not much different than the previous models. Needless to say, these boots did not sell too well as evidenced by the lack of ugly pink boots seen on the slopes in the late 1990s.

In early 2000, the ski industry finally got smart and created boots and skis for women that factored in their unique physical needs and personal desires. Women are generally physically lighter than men and have a lower center of gravity. Therefore, the skis were made of lighter material and the boot bindings were set slightly forward to account for a woman's physicality. The boots were cut a little wider around the calf since women generally have larger calves than men. Equipment was made for beginners as well as for intermediate and advanced skiers and came in a variety of colors. When these skis and boots hit the market, it exploded. Once the ski industry really understood what female skiers wanted and how best to serve them, the sales followed.

These two stories remind me of one of my favorite marketing sayings: "Pink is not a strategy." In her book *Why She Buys: The New Strategy for Reaching the World's Most Powerful Consumers*, Bridget Brennan makes this statement and then backs it up with tons of research and real-life case scenarios from the advertising world. I highly recommend this book, if you want to learn more about marketing and selling to women.

So if female-friendly marketing is not changing the colors on your website to pink and purple, what does it entail? To be female friendly, you need to approach your marketing, messaging, and branding in a way that resonates with real women. It is based on gender research, but does not reinforce general female stereotypes. It speaks to your ideal female client and in many cases also her partner. It highlights how you want to understand her individual financial concerns, listen to her story, and work with her to find solutions.

Female-friendly marketing is not transactional; it is relational. It involves selling less and connecting more. It shows that you and your firm are competent, empathetic, and warm. Good women's marketing invites the female client to have a relationship based on trust and her unique set of life circumstances. Affluent women are intelligent and astute consumers making good female-friendly marketing more of an art than a science. But if you pay attention to how women think, feel, and want to relate to their advisors, then you are on the right path toward a productive marketing campaign.

Define Your Ideal Female Client

The first step in developing a sound marketing strategy is to identify your ideal female client. Ideal clients typically are the ones whom you love working with, who value your expertise, who appreciate your approach to financial planning and investing, and who pay you what you are worth without complaining about your fees. One person's perfect client may be another advisor's nightmare, so know that there is no right answer, just your answer.

As you have already learned, affluent women come in many shapes and sizes. These clients are corporate executives, entrepreneurs, stay-at-home mothers, inheritors, and wealth creators. They are different ages and races, and have different money personalities. Due to this diversity, you need to make sure that your marketing efforts are specifically targeting the type of affluent women you want to attract to your practice. You must be able to see this ideal female client in high definition. If you don't, you run the risk of alienating her by using overarching stereotypes about women that may or may not be true for her. Find a niche within this larger group and focus your message on what resonates with these women. As the old adage goes, know your audience.

The following is a series of questions to help you put your ideal female client into sharp focus. As you look through these

---

In Her Own Words

Don't attempt to target all women with the same messaging and services, ignoring the fact that there are many different types of women with completely different needs who are looking for a variety of services depending on their situation.
—Eileen O'Connor, CFP, coauthor, Women and Wealth: Why Does the Financial Services Industry Still Not Hear Them

questions, notice how they require you to go beyond net worth, income, and investable assets. While these may be useful measures for you in creating a sustainable business, your clients, especially your female ones, are not motivated to hire you based on these financial benchmarks. In fact, promoting your services based on required assets under management is not very client-centric and should be avoided unless it is important to your niche. Instead, invest the time in building a three-dimensional picture of your ideal female client because this ultimately is more successful than trying to reach out to the "female market."

Snapshot: Your Ideal Female Client

1. My ideal female client is best described as . . . .
2. She lives, works, and plays . . . .
3. Three key characteristics she possesses include . . . .
4. She belongs to the following organizations/clubs . . . .
5. Her main financial concerns are . . . .
6. Her main nonfinancial concerns are . . . .
7. I can solve her financial problems by . . . .
8. I can solve her nonfinancial problems by . . . .
9. I am a good match for her because . . . .
10. She should work with me instead of my competition because . . . .

Now take a minute to review your answers and write up a brief description of your ideal client below:

_____

_____

_____

_____

_____

_____

_____

Next, review your book of business and ask yourself, "How many of these ideal female clients do I already work with?" If you have some of these clients already in your practice, ask yourself these questions:

What else do I notice about these women that can help me continue to define my ideal client?

Are these women members of a couple, or are they single, widowed, divorced, or going through some other type of transition?

Are they career professionals, stay-at-home moms, or women working in the family business?

What personality characteristics do they possess?

Are they loud and outspoken, quiet and demure, or just the right mix of both?

What else makes these women easy to connect with and work with?

Jot down what you discover.

The end result of the ideal client exercise is a very specific description of what type of women you want to connect and work with in your practice. The more you know about them, the easier it will be to market to them successfully.

Solve Her Problems

Now that you know who your ideal female client is, it is time to discover her problems and how you can be part of the solution.

Take a minute and consider what keeps her up at night. List what financial worries, pains, and circumstances she might find herself facing. If she is the owner of a family business, she may need family business consulting. If she is a third generation inheritor, she may need assistance with family governance and intergenerational wealth conversations. If she is a career professional, she may want education about how best to invest her 401(k) plan and how to negotiate for a bigger bonus. Whatever her particular problems, you need to figure out how you can provide the skills, support, and resources to help her navigate this part of her financial life. When you do, then it is time to craft a marketing message that speaks to her and her only.

An effective way to find out about your ideal female client's typical concerns is to ask your existing female clients who fit the criteria. By inquiring, you are showing your current female client that you are interested in serving her better and that you are interested in working with more women like her. This makes her feel appreciated and also may aid her in considering you as a potential referral source for her friends and colleagues.

Another method for gathering the data is to invite a small group of women who represent your target market to participate in a focus group. Invite them to a complimentary breakfast or lunch, and facilitate a discussion about their top financial concerns. Be transparent about your purpose, and don't turn this event into a sales pitch since this will just alienate most women.

A Word of Caution: Selling to Affluent Women

The easiest way to lose a potential female client is to channel Dan Aykroyd's slick Super Bass-O-Matic 76 pitchman as you approach her. This classic *Saturday Night Live* skit was hilarious because it hit a chord with all of us. Everyone has met at least one fast-talking, cheesy salesman like Aykroyd's character: the salesman who is so committed to moving product and making a quick buck that he will do or say anything to close the deal. This is the exact type of approach that turns women off (and most clients, for that matter) and gives financial advisors a bad name. It is transactional-based, not client-centric and akin to shooting ducks in a pond. When duck hunting, there is one purpose—to make the kill. The hunter is not sitting in the blind to begin a long-term relationship with his feathery friends, just to shoot one and bring it home for dinner. Advisors who treat selling like hunting are exactly what women don't want. Remember, no one likes to be prey.

Talk to Her About Benefits

Now that you know what your ideal female client's concerns are and how you can help, you need to find a way to communicate the benefits of hiring you in all your marketing materials. It is a common mistake for financial services professionals to write marketing copy highlighting features of products and services and not focus on the benefits to the client. Because services and features are pretty generic in the financial advising field, this does not set you apart from the competition. What does distinguish you is how you make clients feel when you provide advice, counsel, and services. This benefit of working with you is unique to you and your firm. Therefore, these benefits should be the focus of all your print, online, and in-person marketing efforts.

Here is an example. A 40-year-old woman and her partner ask you to start a 529 plan for her son's college education. The service you provide is setting up the account and recommending the proper monthly allocation. But what is the benefit to the couple? The benefit is having peace of mind by feeling like a responsible parent and not having to worry about college tuition. Your clients can hire anyone to set up this educational fund. They hired you to provide the nontangible experience of feeling like good parents in establishing the account.

Another example is a financial plan. Most advisors offer a financial plan for an additional onetime fee or as part of their asset under management. The client does not agree to pay for a financial plan because she wants a notebook with your logo on it filled with colored charts and graphs. No, she buys a financial plan to gain clarity, to reduce anxiety, and to feel more comfortable about her family's financial future.

Take a moment to look at your website or to read through your latest company newsletter or brochure. Do you talk about benefits or features? How many times do you reference the services or the features of that service, but neglect to include the benefit to the client in receiving it? As a female-friendly advisor, you need to talk to her about the benefits of working with you, not the features or mechanics of what you do.

Tap into Her Network

You have defined your ideal female client, identified her common financial problems, and can communicate the emotional benefits of hiring you. Now it is time to start networking with her centers of influence and connecting with other female-friendly advisors. By tapping into her network and being referred by someone she already trusts, you gain instant credibility. As Bill Cates, author of *Get More Referrals Now!* and president of Referral Coach International, says, "When you get referrals you're borrowing the trust from the referrer until you can establish your own."

The easiest way to build this network is to find other professionals or centers of influence that currently work with your ideal female client. These may include accountants, bankers, divorce attorneys, family business consultants, estate planning attorneys, executive coaches, family wealth consultants, and mental health professionals. Decide which group to reach out to based on your target market. For instance, if you are interested in advising widows, then consider networking with grief and loss counselors and estate planning attorneys. If you plan on advising more women who own family businesses, then family business consultants and bankers may be more appropriate.

If you are uncertain of the other professionals and networking opportunities in your geographic area, conduct a Google search. Consider searching for any of the professionals listed above and also "women's organizations." Often women's organizations such as the local chapter of the National Association of Women Business Owners or the Women's Bar Association are wonderful venues for finding other professionals who work with your target market. Before attending an event, check to see if both men and women are welcome. If so, go. If the organization is not co-ed, then contact that executive director and find out if you can meet to find out the best way to connect with the members. This may mean being a sponsor of an event, advertising on their website, or becoming a board member.

Occasionally, a male advisor will complain that female-friendly networks tend to be largely made up of women professionals who are not interested in networking with male professionals. While this may be true in some cases, it is often the exception to the rule. Instead many women admire those men who take time to attend events and/or support women's organizations. However, women do take longer to make an initial referral to another professional. Similar to female clients, they need time to develop a trusting relationship first before sending clients your way. But if you are consistent and invest time into collegial relationships, tapping into her network is a very effective female-friendly marketing strategy.

The Dos and Don'ts of Female-Friendly Marketing

The most important thing to remember when marketing to female clients is that this group of women is made up of individuals who are different in a number of ways, even though they are all the same gender. The ideal female clients' exercise is designed to help you drill down into your clients' persona so you will avoid sweeping and often inaccurate generalizations.

The following is a list of dos and don'ts for marketing to affluent women. As you review these tips, keep in mind what is important to your particular ideal client and make changes in your approach accordingly.

Do Have Gender Appeal

In her book *Why She Buys*, Bridget Brennan encourages companies to have gender appeal. This is the type of marketing that resonates strongly with the culture of a particular sex and is very similar to using an advertisement with a generational message that taps into the collective consciousness of those born during a certain time period. Brennan uses the MasterCard Priceless campaign as an example of good gender appeal. This popular ad campaign shares a list of purchases made, the price paid, and the rationale for the purchase price paid. With each item the cost increases and eventually the narrator shares a big ticket item and simply says, "Priceless." This ad copy is directly tied to the behavioral research about how women shop by grazing in a store and often end up with unplanned items that they may need help justifying. Who can't resist the idea of buying something that is priceless? Based on the success of this ad campaign with women, MasterCard got it right.

When marketing to female prospects and clients, you want to keep in mind the common rites of passage and milestones in women's lives, how women communicate, and the images and words that trigger positive responses from them. Women don't want to be reminded of their age, so reference women's life stages in your marketing, not her birthday. As discussed in Chapter 4, "Women in Transition," female clients go through a series of life transitions and each transition has a unique set of challenges and rewards. Use what you have learned in this book to tap into how they can benefit from hiring you to assist them in navigating these developmental events in life.

Do Use Female-Friendly Language

It is common practice for a financial services firm to use male-dominated language in advertising campaigns, websites, and client newsletters. Hundreds of these marketing messages talk about offering sound investment advice aimed at offering a high return on investment and superior portfolio management. In other words, we can beat out the competition and make you more money. This message may resonate with some affluent female clients, but typically it uses very male-centric language that misses the mark with a woman's more holistic view of money and wealth. Be sure to review your marketing materials and eliminate words such as *annihilate, crush, destroy, win,* and *shatter* with language that caters to the female brain. Incorporate words such as *balance, harmony, stability,* and *trustworthy* into your marketing materials because these concepts resonate with women's desires to be connected and work together.

Do Tell Stories

Women, like all clients, remember stories far longer than details and facts. Whenever possible, use storytelling to market your practice. By sharing tales about clients who are in similar situations or have faced comparable financial challenges, you are showing prospects and clients that you understand their needs and have experience advising women like them. Remember, women look for areas to connect to and to feel included in your world. Stories can really help her see that you are the right man (or woman) for the job.

Do Ask for Referrals

Women love to refer their friends, colleagues, relatives, and business associates to professionals that they know and trust. According to Delia Passi, author of the book *Winning the Toughest Customer: The Essential Guide to Selling to Women,* "While the average man takes about two points of contact before you can close the sale with him, the average woman takes about five to seven." But once she does sign on, she is very loyal and likely to make over two dozen referrals to you over her lifetime. Unlike men, women rely more on word-of-mouth referrals from friends and confidantes than on concrete data. Therefore, one of the best marketing strategies is for you to be an excellent female-friendly advisor, a resource to her for both her financial and personal life and someone she would call a friend.

Do Use Social Media

Social media speaks to the female brain, culture, and desire for a sense of community. According to a Nielsen study released in 2010, women are the majority of users of social networking sites and spend 30 percent more time on these sites than men do.[2] Women like to connect, and when they are too busy to see each other in person, saying hello via Facebook, Twitter, or LinkedIn fulfills this need.

The financial industry has been slow to embrace social media as a valid business development practice, citing compliance concerns as the reason. However, the Internet and social media sites are here to stay and are tools for gathering data about your ideal female client and interfacing with her on a regular basis. Going forward, clients are going to expect advisors to be online and available through social media, especially for the next generation clients who use Facebook as their primary mode of communication. Invest the time now in learning how to capitalize on this medium, and incorporate it into your overall marketing strategy. A great resource on this topic is Wired Advisor, a company started by Stephanie Sammons, a former regional sales manager for a global financial services firm. The website, http://www.wiredadvisor.com, offers up-to-date information about regulations and best practices for financial advisors.

Don't Be Sexist

This one seems like a no-brainer. But you want to tread lightly when it comes to making sexist comments, telling racy jokes, or giving the appearance of being a male chauvinist. Many women enjoy edgy humor, don't mind being called "girl," and find raunchy jokes entertaining. The problem is you never know who these women are and who they are not. So err on the side of caution, watch your language, and don't do anything that can be perceived as sexist.

Don't Tell Her What She Already Knows

Have you ever seen the advertisement for Sure Deodorant Motionsense System? The copy reads like this: "Sure asked women to use these jingle bells for one entire day so they realize how much they move." When I first saw this commercial, I was insulted. Do they really think women are too dumb to know how much they move? With each viewing, I became more and more dumbfounded. How could a deodorant company think this ad would be effective with women? Did the ad executives really think that their female customers were unaware of their busy lives and needed bells tied to their wrists and ankles to remind them of how much they moved in a 24-hour period of time? Women already know how busy they are and don't need to be reminded by hearing bells throughout the day! Being a female is equal to being overscheduled and overworked and the last thing a woman wants is a bell tied around her neck like the family dog to remind her.

This commercial breaks one of the fundamental rules for marketing to women. Don't tell your female customers what they already know. Women know how busy they are, how much they have to accomplish in a day, and how much they move around to complete tasks before the sun goes down. They are not interested in seeing the crazy pace of the typical female day in print advertisements and marketing campaigns. What women want are solutions aimed at reducing the frantic pace of life. Your female clients want to know you have services and financial tools to make taking care of their family finances more efficient. Make sure your web copy, marketing message, and sales approach clearly communicate the benefit of working with you, not something she already knows about her own life.

Don't Fake It

Women know when you are not being real and truthful. This instinct is often called "a woman's intuition," and it is incredibly accurate. If you are going to market to women, do so in a way that shows that you care and that you really have her best interest at heart. In writing this book, I heard countless stories from women who met with advisors who gave lip service to being interested in advising them only to end up not really listening or caring about their needs. This is not how women operate, so be authentic, real, and transparent in all your marketing communication, and whatever you do, don't fake it!

Don't Sell, Connect

Affluent women are bombarded with salespeople wanting to buy products and services. An aggressive sales pitch that comes on too strong is bound to turn them off. Instead of selling to them, focus your efforts on connecting and building a relationship. As you have learned, relationship selling speaks to women and is their preferred way of doing business with you. Invest the time in attending network-

IN HER OWN WORDS

I was really turned off when a financial advisor who wanted to get into our networking group pursued a business relationship with me. The minute he was accepted as a group member, he couldn't give me the time of day. I felt betrayed as I thought he really was interested in helping me. It turns out he just wanted to help himself.

—DYLAN, 44-YEAR-OLD MARRIED ENTREPRENEUR

ing events, hosting luncheons, and finding ways to meet with your women clients one-on-one. This type of connection is not only good for your marketing and public relations, it builds the foundation for enrolling more female clients who are loyal and top-notch referrers.

Now that you have some rules to guide you in developing or revamping your female-friendly marketing, let's take a look at some tactical tools you can use to begin reaching out to women in a meaningful and effective way.

Female-Friendly Marketing Tactics

It is time to get the word out that you are a female-friendly advisor. Below are some of my favorite marketing tools for reaching out to women. Review the list, and select the projects that speak to your strengths and delegate or leave the others behind. Remember, a few well-executed and consistent marketing efforts are more effective than numerous ones that miss the mark.

Write a Female-Friendly Client Article

Consider writing an article on a financial problem that is interesting to women. Topics such as how to raise affluent children, how to talk with your husband about money, and how to protect your family's assets all play well with female clients. Keep the articles short and interesting, using stories whenever possible. Before it goes to print, have a female colleague or client review the article to measure its gender appeal. Next, select the publications your ideal female client is most likely to read. Don't be intimidated since local newspapers, trade magazines, and online media outlets are constantly looking for good content.

Once the article is published, share it with your clients and colleagues. If you have not signed an exclusive copyright agreement with the publication, post it on your website as a resource and/or reprint it in your newsletter. One well-written article can go a long way in establishing your credibility as a female-friendly and knowledgeable advisor.

Speak at a Women's Business Conference

If you are a good speaker, or aspire to be one, consider putting your name in the hat to speak at a women's business conference in your area. Based on your preferred niche, these venues can offer you access to a room full of ideal female clients all at once. Not only is this an effective use of your marketing time, it demonstrates that you are committed to taking action to help businesswomen live healthier financial lives.

In putting together your presentation, it is important that you keep it educational. Nothing turns off a group of women more quickly than a 45-minute sales pitch. As with the article, consider the topics that are relevant to the audience and use your expertise to raise the audience's awareness about this topic.

The best speakers speak from the heart, so pick a topic that you are passionate about and can bring to life on stage. Some male advisors invite a female colleague to share the spotlight. This can make for an interesting presentation, but it is not mandatory. By partnering with a female advisor, you are demonstrating to the audience how you interact with a woman firsthand and that you believe both sexes have value to add to the discussion.

If you are new to presenting, hire a speech coach to help you fine-tune your message and work on your delivery. Or, if you prefer not to present, hire a topic expert and sponsor this speaker at the conference. This can reduce your stress level while making a big impact on the audience. Professional speakers work full-time to be effective and entertaining presenters.

Host a Women, Wine, and Wealth Event

Offer a women, wine, and wealth event at your office. Invite a small group of women, 20 or less, to enjoy an evening with you and taste wine. Keep the event light and social. You may want to talk for a few minutes, but remember the purpose of the event is to build your relationship with your current clients and foster new ones.

Don't know much about wine? You don't need to worry. Wine consultants will come in and set up the entire wine tasting, serve as experts, and take the pressure off you so you can mingle as you wish.

If a wine tasting is not a good theme for your ideal female client, consider some alternatives that are more likely to resonate with her. Play off national holidays, such as Valentine's Day, Mother's Day, and/or Independence Day. Make it more general by hosting a Client Appreciation Day. What is most important is that you demonstrate through your actions that you care enough to make her feel special.

Sponsor a Women's Golf, Tennis, or Ski Tournament

Many affluent women are active and enjoy sports just as much as men do. So why not sponsor a golf, tennis, or ski tournament? You can create your own or piggy back on one already established by a women's organization. Often sports clubs and ski mountains are set up to run events and can help you with coordinating the day. Pick a location that is convenient for the majority of your female clients and prospects so they can more easily build this event into their typically overscheduled day. Offer complimentary pro lessons, a nice lunch, and cocktails at the end of the day. Tournaments create an atmosphere of camaraderie and trust. By hosting or sponsoring this type of event, you are showing female clients that you believe women are worthy of playing with too.

Sponsor a Raising Financially Responsible Children Seminar

The number one concern of affluent parents is how to best raise children of privilege; therefore, seminars aimed at alleviating this fear and providing sound parent tools are a great success. Consider making this event co-ed, but know that you may get more women attending than men.

There are firms, such as Independent Means, Inc., and Gallo Consulting, LLC, that offer financial literacy training for high-net-worth families. These organizations make great partners when planning this type of seminar. Consider hosting a panel of experts on the topic with you as the moderator. This approach demonstrates that you are a team player, are connected to resources on this topic, and are open to discussing this issue with your clients.

A great idea is to give your clients a book on financial literacy at the end of the event, personally signed by you. It is a useful tool for your clients and a friendly reminder that you not only care about their financial health but the well-being of their children and grandchildren as well. Refer to the Female-Friendly Resource Guide at the back of the book for ideas on books to gift.

Partner with a Charitable Cause

Affluent women are big supporters of philanthropy and charitable work. If you share this passion for giving back, this is a wonderful way to meet more of your ideal female clients and connect with them authentically. Nonprofit organizations are always looking for financially savvy professionals to serve on boards, so they are receptive to having you help out. If you don't have time to commit fully to a board of directors position, consider partnering with a nonprofit organization on a project or event. Sponsor a table at a gala, showcase upcoming artist work in your office, or ask local charities if you can write articles for their newsletters.

Create a Female-Friendly Resource Guide

Take time to create a list of resources for your ideal female clients. Start by reviewing the Female-Friendly Resource Guide at the back of this book. Then add websites, books, articles, videos, and podcasts of your own. Share this list with the women in your practice either by sending it out by mail or by handing it out at the next client meeting. Also post it on your website as a resource for prospects to review as well as current clients to refer back to as needed.

Women pride themselves on being a source of help and a resource to others. By providing them with an updated resource list, you are making their ability to care for others easier, which is a win-win for you and them.

Share Your Expertise Using Social Media and Video

With technology being so user-friendly these days, it is fairly easy to start a radio show, engage in a social media discussion group, or post a video online. Communication via the Internet to your preferred clients is a great way to bring your message and personality alive. It is also a great tool for delivering a large amount of content quickly and for enticing your audience to stay on your website longer. One minute of video equals 1.8 million words. In other words, you can deliver the equivalent of three pages of text in a single video frame.[3] Not only does video help you say more, clients listen longer. According to research conducted by YouTube TV, the average website viewer spends only 48 seconds on a traditional text website; however, when video is added, this jumps to five minutes and 50 seconds.[4] Of course you need to check with your compliance department to determine the restrictions on your use of these tools, but the evidence is clear: social media and video are powerful marketing vehicles.

Summary

Marketing to affluent women is very similar to marketing to any group of potential clients. First you need to clearly define your ideal client. Don't make the mistake of putting female clients into a group labeled "the female market." Instead, take the time to really get to know her by using the exercises and strategies offered in this chapter. Communicate your value in terms of benefits to her and her family. And make sure that all your marketing materials speak to her and accurately reflect the service you provide.

Your Next Step: Female-Friendly Marketing Review

Gather all you collateral materials, including recent advertising and public relations campaigns, print brochures, client newsletters, articles and publications, and web copy. Now review each marketing piece, asking the following questions:

1. Does the copy of this marketing piece communicate the key benefits to my ideal female clients? If not, what corrective action is needed?

2. Do the design, images, and colors used for this marketing piece resonate with my ideal female clients? If not, what corrective action is needed?

3. Do the different marketing pieces incorporate female-oriented language and address financial and other concerns relevant to my ideal female clients? If not, what corrective action is needed?

4. What do I need to change in my overall marketing strategy and branding to speak more to my ideal female clients?

5. What do I do well and need to continue doing when it comes to marketing to my ideal female clients?

Once you have answered these five questions for yourself, ask five of your most trusted female clients or colleagues who represent your ideal target market to answer them as well. Once each of these women has submitted written answers to you, find a time that is mutually convenient for them to come in for a focus group discussion. This session should last no longer than 90 minutes and should be facilitated by someone other than yourself, if possible. At a minimum, have someone in the room to take notes so you can focus solely on the feedback and not be concerned with documentation. It is important in this meeting to just listen to the focus group participants and not try to defend your past marketing decisions. Later you will evaluate all the ideas shared in the focus group session and decide which concepts you will incorporate into your marketing strategy going forward. For example, you may leave this group session with 10 new ideas, but select only one or two to implement. A good structure for this group is to let each member talk for 10 minutes about her impressions, then allow 5 minutes for the other focus group members to ask questions or brainstorm ideas. When 15 minutes passes, the next person starts her critique. This type of structure will allow all members to be heard and understood, so the last 15 minutes of the 90-minute meeting can be spent brainstorming next steps.

After the meeting, take time to review the notes from the meeting and to reflect on what your focus group members share with you. Act on the feedback that resonates with you and your target market and leave the other ideas behind. The question you want to answer is: "What needs to change to attract more of my ideal female clients, and what is working that should stay the same?" You may need a complete overhaul or just a touch up in how you are marketing to women. Whatever the outcome, develop a plan for changing your marketing message over the next year, checking in with your ideal female clients for their feedback regularly.

Afterword

Writing this book has strengthened my belief in the importance of working to bridge the gap between financial advisors and affluent women. Through countless interviews and conversations with these women, I learned of their struggles to find an advisor who is competent and caring. I also discovered how many good financial advisors, male and female, are out there who truly want to do the best by their female clients. Although there is a gap between what women want and what the financial services industry provides, it can be filled with education, training, and mentoring. Any financial advisor who wants to learn these skills can learn them. As I tell most people, my work is not rocket science. It is simply about how to have a healthy professional relationship that includes communicating effectively and understanding clients on a deeper human level.

There were a few things I discovered when writing this book that are worth sharing here as they can inform your work too. First, affluent women are reluctant to openly talk about money and wealth. While intellectually I know money is a taboo subject in our society, actually meeting up with this taboo was both disconcerting and eye opening. As women, we have economic power, but we tend to downplay it. Even friends and colleagues who share intimate details of their lives with me clammed up when I asked them to talk about their affluence. Some women did not consider themselves to be wealthy; others knew, but wanted it to remain a secret. I, too, struggled with my assumptions about women, money, and my worthiness to be writing this book. Money represents so much more than dollars and cents, and in this interviewing process it was crystal clear that women have more work to do on being open and accepting of themselves and their financial status. This work certainly can be facilitated by you, the advisor.

Second, I was struck by how many male financial advisors truly care about women. These men were not the stereotypical fast-talking, money-driven advisors you read about in the media. Instead, they were compassionate and heartfelt, and really enjoyed advising affluent female clients. Collectively, they demonstrated patience, a love for education, and a true desire to help women navigate the complex financial landscape involved in being a wife, mother, and daughter. These men reported more meaningful relationships with their female clients and viewed them as the catalysts for families to proactively financially plan for the future. Some even preferred to work with women rather than men, finding women to be more receptive to advice and more forthcoming with referrals. I believe these men are unsung heroes and need to be more readily recognized in the field as doing good work while also being savvy businessmen.

Last, I wondered what the next generation of affluent women and financial advisors will look like. Will female clients be less reluctant to talk about their economic power and more apt to speak up in advising meetings when their needs are not getting met? Will the next generation of financial advisors stop making the assumption that men have the power and women are not interested in financial and wealth management? Or will they make the same mistakes the industry has historically made when it comes to balancing women's needs with men's? Only time will tell. But certainly my work is part of a growing trend addressing the needs of affluent women, their increased wealth, and how financial advisors can respond and capitalize on the opportunity to serve them. I am proud to be part of this movement and hope you will jump on board as well. Together we can change the industry to be more female friendly. With a little teamwork, female clients can stop declaring that financial advisors don't listen and start bragging about how well their advisors do.

Any financial advisor who wants to learn the essential skills for advising affluent women can. You don't need to have a female brain or be an expert in women psychology; all you need is the ability to listen. Really listen to your female clients as individuals and as members of a couple. Take the extra step to understand their perspectives. Don't assume they are like all the other women you see. Admit when you don't know or need further clarification. Be patient because their decision-making process may be slower, but remember that it is just as valid as yours. They need you and you need them. And isn't that what a good working relationship is all about?

Notes

Introduction

1. J. Havens and P. Schervish, "Why the $41 Trillion Wealth Transfer Estimate Is Still Valid: A Review of Challenges and Questions," *Journal of Gift Planning*, vol. 7, no. 1, January 2003, pp. 11–15, 47–50.
2. H. Pordeli and P. Wynkoop, *The Economic Impact of Women-Owned Businesses in the United States*, Research Report, Center for Women's Business Research, McLean, VA, October 2009; and *Key Facts About Women-Owned Businesses (2008–2009)*, http://www.womensbusinessresearchcenter.org/research/keyfacts/.
3. Pordeli and Wynkoop, *The Economic Impact of Women-Owned Businesses in the United States*.

Chapter 1

1. K. Wojnar and C. Meek, "Women's Views of Wealth and the Planning Process: It's Their Values That Matter, Not Just Their Value," *Advisor Perspectives*, 2011, http://www.advisorperspectives.com.
2. "New State Farm Study Examines What It Takes to Earn Women's Trust," Press Release, State Farm, Bloomingdale, IL, August 6, 2008, http://www.statefarm.com/aboutus/_pressreleases/2008/womens_trust_study.asp.
3. M. Silverstein, K. Kato, and P. Tischhauser, *Women Want More: How to Capture Your Share of the World's Largest, Fastest Growing Market*, New York: HarperBusiness, 2009.
4. "Hot Topics: Women and Philanthropy, Sharing the Wealth," *To the Contrary* hosted by Bonnie Erbe, PBS Online, http://www.pbs.org/ttc/headlines_economics_philanthropy.html.
5. B. Brennan, *Why She Buys: The New Strategy for Reaching the World's Most Powerful Consumers*, New York: Crown Business, 2009, p. 4.
6. "Research Reveals Affluent Women Taking Control of Their Wealth," *Trusts & Estates*, May 5, 2009, http://trustsandestates.com/press_release/aflluent-women-taking-wealth-control-0505/.
7. *Key Facts About Women-Owned Businesses (2008–2009)*, http://www.womensbusinessresearchcenter.org/research/keyfacts/.
8. H. Pordeli and P. Wynkoop, *The Economic Impact of Women-Owned Businesses in the United States*, Research Report, Center for Women's Business Research, McLean, VA, October 2009.
9. "Women in Financial Services" (Fact Sheet), Catalyst, April 2012, http://www.catalyst.org/file/592/qt_women_in_financial_services.pdf.
10. B. Kay and A. DiLeonardi, *$14 Trillion Women: Your Essential Guide to Engaging the Female Client*, Self-Published, p. 100.
11. L. Brizendine, *The Female Brain*, New York: Broadway, 2006.

12. Staff Writer, "2011 100 Most Influential People in Finance," *Treasury and Risk*, June 1, 2011, http://www.treasuryandrisk.com/2011/06/01/2011-100-most-influential-people-in-finance.

13. A. Laurence, J. Maltby, and J. Rutterford, *Women and Their Money 1700–1950: Essays on Women and Finance*, New York: Routledge, 2009.

14. Ibid.

15. Ibid.

16. "Hot Topics: Women and Philanthropy, Sharing the Wealth."

17. Allianz Life Insurance, *Report on Women, Money and Power*, Minneapolis: Allianz, 2006.

18. A. Lusardi, "Women and Finance," *International Business Times*, April 1, 2010, http://www.ibtimes.com/contents/20100401/women-finance.htm.

Chapter 2

1. K. Wojnar and C. Meek, "Women's Views of Wealth and the Planning Process: It's Their Values That Matter, Not Just Their Value," *Advisor Perspectives*, 2011, http://www.advisorperspectives.com.

2. D. Passi, *Winning the Toughest Customer: The Essential Guide to Selling to Women*, Chicago: Kaplan Publishing, 2006.

3. C. Gilligan, *In a Different Voice*, Boston: Harvard University Press, 1993.

4. L. Brizendine, *The Female Brain*, New York: Broadway, 2006.

5. J. Zweig, *Your Money & Your Brain: How the New Science of Neuroeconomics Can Help Make You Rich*, New York: Simon & Schuster, 2007.

6. Women & Co., *Women and Affluence 2010: The Era of Financial Responsibility*, Citicorp, August 2009.

7. L. Davidson, L. Robertson, N. Anderson, and G. Ward, "2011 Research Financial Stress," Financial Finesse, Inc., 2011, http://www.pfeef.org/research/2011-Financial-Stress-Research.pdf.

8. National Alliance of Caregiving and AARP, Caregiving in the United States, Report, November 2009, http://www.caregiving.org/data/Caregiving_in_the_US_2009_full_report.pdf.

9. Met Life, "Study of Caregiving Costs to Working Caregivers," 2011, http://www.guardianship.org/reports/mmi_caregiving_costs_working_caregivers.pdf.

10. Anonymous, "Mattel Says It Erred; Teen Talk Barbie Turns Silent on Math," *New York Times*, October 21, 1992, http://www.nytimes.com/1992/10/21/business/company-news-mattel-says-it-erred-teen-talk-barbie-turns-silent-on-math.html.

11. M. Bombardieri, "Summers' Remarks on Women Draw Fire," *Boston Globe*, January 17, 2005, http://www.boston.com/news/local/articles/2005/01/17/summers_remarks_on_women_draw_fire/.

12. M. Szalavitz, "The Math Gender Gap: Nurture Trumps Nature," *Time Healthland*, August 30, 2011, http://healthland.time.com/2011/08/30/

the-math-gender-gap-nurture-can-trump-nature/.

13. B. Brennan, *Why She Buys: The New Strategy for Reaching the World's Most Powerful Consumers*, New York: Crown Business, 2009, p. 4.

14. A. Benson, Personal Interview, October 28, 2011.

15. A. Laurence, J. Maltby, and J. Rutterford, *Women and Their Money 1700–1950: Essays on Women and Finance*, New York: Routledge, 2009.

16. B. Barber and T. Odean, "Boys Will Be Boys: Gender, Overconfidence and Common Stock Investment," *The Quarterly Journal of Economics*, vol. 116, issue 1, February 2001, p. 261–292.

17. Women & Co., *Women and Affluence 2010*.

18. "Research Reveals Affluent Women Taking Control of Their Wealth," *Trusts & Estates*, May 5, 2009, http://trustsandestates.com/press_release/affluent-women-taking-wealth-control-0505/.

19. Prudential Research Group, *Financial Experience & Behaviors Around Women*, Newark, NJ: Prudential, 2010.

20. "Women in Financial Services" (Fact Sheet), Catalyst, April 2012, http://www.catalyst.org/file/592/qt_women_in_financial_services.pdf.

Chapter 3

1. R. Arora and L. Saad, "Marketing to Mass Affluent Women," *Gallop Management Journal*, March 2005, http://gmj.gallup.com/content/15196/Marketing-Mass-Affluent-Women.aspx.

2. K. Rosplock, *Women and Wealth: Executive Summary and Key Findings*, Research Report, GenSpring Family Offices, 2007.

3. R. Prince and H. Grove, *Women of Wealth: Understanding Today's Affluent Female Investor*, Cincinnati: The National Underwriter Company, 2004.

4. J. Grubman and D. Jaffe, "Immigrants and Natives to Wealth: Understanding Clients Based on Their Wealth Origins," *Journal of Financial Planning*, vol. 20, issue 6, July 2007, pp. 46–54.

5. D. Kindoln, "Too Much of a Good Thing—Raising Children of Character in an Indulgent Age," Presentation sponsored by the Boston Estate Planning Council, Boston, MA, October 20, 2010.

6. Allianz Life Insurance, *Report on Women, Money and Power*, Minneapolis: Allianz, 2006.

7. Ibid.

8. U.S. Department of Education, *The Condition of Education 2011*, The National Center for Education Statistics, 2011.

9. H. Pordeli and P. Wynkoop, *The Economic Impact of Women-Owned Businesses in the United States*, White Paper, Center for Women's Business Research, McLean, VA, October 2009; and *Key Facts About Women-Owned Businesses (2008–2009)*, http://www.womensbusinessresearchcenter.org/research/keyfacts/.

10. B. Friedan, *The Feminine Mystique*, 35th Anniversary Edition, New York:

W.W. Norton & Co., Inc. 1997.

11. *The White House Project: Benchmarking Women's Leadership*, Key Findings Report, Washington: The White House Project, 2009.
12. Ibid.
13. The Center on Philanthropy at Indiana University, "The 2011 Study of High Net Worth: Women's Philanthropy and the Impact of Women Giving Networks," Bank of America, December 2011.
14. Rosplock, *Women and Wealth.*
15. Ledbury Research, *Tomorrow's Philanthropist*, Report, London: Barclay's Wealth, 2009.
16. A. Slomski, "Women and Money," *Merrill Lynch Advisor Magazine*, Spring 2011, pp. 6–11.
17. Ibid.
18. "Silver Bridge Advisors, A Woman's Perspective: Health and Wealth," Presentation, Boston, MA, April 12, 2011.
19. *The Impact of Retirement Risk on Women*, Research Report, Washington: Society of Actuaries and the Women Institute for Secure Retirement, December 2010.
20. Slomski, "Women and Money."

Chapter 4

1. K. Wojnar and C. Meek, "Women's Views of Wealth and the Planning Process: It's Their Values That Matter, Not Just Their Value," *Advisor Perspectives*, 2011, http://www.advisorperspectives.com; and *The Impact of Retirement Risk on Women*, Research Report, Washington: Society of Actuaries and the Women Institute for Secure Retirement, December 2010.
2. M. Anthony, *Your Clients for Life: The Definitive Guide to Becoming a Successful Financial Planner,* Second Edition, Chicago: Dearborn Trade Publishing, 2005.
3. J. Quattlebaum, Personal Interview, December 5, 2011.
4. C. Washburn and D. Christen, "Financial Harmony: A Key Component of Successful Marriage Relationship," *The Forum for Family and Consumer Issues*, vol. 13, Spring 2008.
5. E. Kubler-Ross, *On Death and Dying*, New York: Touchstone, 1969.
6. K. Rehl, Personal Interview, January 31, 2012.

Chapter 6

1. C. Anderson and D. Sharpe, Communication Issues in Life Planning: Defining Key Factors in Developing Successful Planner-Client Relationships, Financial Planning Association, White Paper, 2008.

Chapter 7

1. Allianz Life Insurance, *Report on Women, Money and Power*, Minneapolis: Allianz, 2006.
2. E. Blayney, "Empowering, Educating, and Engaging Women Clients," *The Journal of Financial Planning*, vol. 23, issue 10, October 2010, p. 48–55.
3. Prudential Research Group, "Financial Experience & Behaviors Around Women," Newark, NJ: Prudential, 2010.
4. A. Slomski, "Women and Money," *Merrill Lynch Advisor Magazine*, Spring 2011, pp. 6–11.
5. J. Flynn, K. Heath, and D. Holt, "Four Ways Women Stunt Their Careers Unintentionally," *Harvard Business Review*, October 19, 2011.
6. B. Klontz and T. Klontz, *Mind Over Money: Overcoming the Money Disorders That Threaten Our Financial Health*, New York: Crown Business, 2009.
7. B. Stanny, *Overcoming Underearning: A Five-Step Plan to a Richer Life*, New York: HarperCollins, 2005.
8. *The White House Project: Benchmarking Women's Leadership,* Key Findings Report, Washington: The White House Project, 2009.
9. L. Babcock and S. Laschever, *Women Don't Ask: The High Cost of Avoiding Negotiation and Positive Strategies for Change*, New York: Bantam Books, 2007.

Chapter 8

1. "Hot Topics: Women and Philanthropy, Sharing the Wealth," *To the Contrary* hosted by Bonnie Erbe, PBS Online, http://www.pbs.org/ttc/headlines_economics_philanthropy.html.
2. B. Brennan, *Why She Buys: The New Strategy for Reaching the World's Most Powerful Consumers*, New York: Crown Business, 2009, p. 4.
3. O. Mellan, "The Evolution of Money Harmony Work," Financial Therapy Association Annual Conference, Keynote Address, Athens, GA, September 12, 2011.

Chapter 9

1. R. Williams and V. Preisser, *Preparing Heirs: Five Steps to a Successful Transition of Family Wealth and Values*, San Francisco: Robert Reed Publishers, 2010.
2. Allianz Life Insurance, *American Legacies Study*, Minneapolis: Allianz, 2005.
3. Women & Co., *Women and Affluence 2010: The Era of Financial Responsibility*, Survey Report New York: Citicorp, August 2009.
4. L. Rosen, "iGeneration Psychology: Parenting and Relating to Our

Tech-Savvy Youth," Online Course, Sonoma, CA: Zur Institute, December 23, 2011.

5. M. Colgan, "Get Practical and Personal with Estate Planning—It Is Not Just the Money That Matters," *Journal of Practical Estate Planning*, vol. 10, issue 6, December 2008–January 2009, pp. 37–42.

6. *2011 World Wealth Report*, Pennington, NJ: Merrill Lynch Wealth Management and Capgemini Consulting, 2011.

7. J. Godfrey, *Raising Financially Fit Kids*, New York: Ten Speed Press, 2003.

8. J. Grubman, "Evolving Your Practice to Serve the Next Generation of High-Net-Worth Families," White Paper, Boston, MA, Pioneer Investments, 2009.

Chapter 10

1. F. Miller and E. Gray, "LEGO Friends Petition: Parents, Women and Girls Ask Toy Companies to Stop Gender-Based Marketing," *Huffington Post*, January 15, 2012.

2. L. Abraham, M. Morn, and A. Vollman, "Women and the Web: How Women Are Shaping the Internet," White Paper, ComScore, Inc., June 2010, http://www.comscore.com/Press_Events/Presentations_Whitepapers/2010/Women_on_the_Web_How_Women_are_Shaping_the_Internet; and A.Lee, "Why Women Rule the Internet," guest post, TechCrunch, AOL Tech, March 20, 2011, http://techcrunch.com/2011/03/20/why-women-rule-the-internet/.

3. C. Pannunzio, "Use Video to Connect with Clients," *Investment News*, February 13, 2012.

4. Ibid.

Female-Friendly Resource Guide

The following are female-friendly resources categorized by topic. These books, organizations, and online resources provide useful information for you and your female clients.

Business
Books

Ask for It
By Linda Babcock and Sara Laschever
This book teaches readers why negotiation is challenging for women and offers a four-phase program, backed by years of research, on how to identify what you're really worth and develop a strategy to make the money you deserve.

Knowing Your Value: Women, Money and Getting What You're Worth
By Mika Brzezinski
This book provides an in-depth look at how women today achieve their deserved recognition and financial worth. Through interviews of prominent women and men, Brzezinski reveals why women are paid less and the pitfalls women face when trying to get their worth at work while trying to move up in their field.

Women in Family Business: What Keeps You Up at Night?
By Patricia M. Annino, Thomas Davidow, Lisbeth Davidow, and Cynthia Adams Harrison
The authors, well-known experts in the field, address the psychological, relational, and financial issues impacting women in family-owned businesses.

Organizations

Center for Women's Business Research
http://www.womensbusinessresearchcenter.org
The Center for Women's Business Research provides rigorous data-driven knowledge that advances the economic, social, and political impact of women business owners and their enterprises.

The National Association of Women Business Owners (NAWBO)
http://www.nawbo.org
This organization is a resource for propelling women business owners into greater economic, social, and political spheres worldwide. NAWBO prides itself on being

a global beacon for influence, ingenuity, and action and is uniquely positioned to provide incisive commentary on issues of importance to women business owners.

Financial Confidence and Education
Books

Money Shy to Money Sure: A Woman's Road Map to Financial Well-Being
by Olivia Mellan and Sherry Christie
The authors of this book analyze the seven most common myths that hamper women when dealing with money and then counter those misconceptions with positive messages based on facts.

On My Own Two Feet: A Modern Girl's Guide to Personal Finance
by Manisha Thakor and Sharon Kedar
Through the use of their financial planning experience, Thakor and Kedar teach young women what they need to know about saving and investing in language that is user-friendly.

Prince Charming Isn't Coming, Revised Edition
by Barbara Stanny
When this groundbreaking yet compassionate book was first published 10 years ago, it lifted a veil on women's resistance to managing their money, revealing that many were still waiting for a prince to rescue them financially. In this revised edition, which reflects our present-day economic world, the author inspires readers to take charge of their money and their lives.

The Secrets of Six-Figure Women
by Barbara Stanny
This book explores the traits of financially successful women and offers practical guidance to those women who aspire to increase their wealth.

Women's Worth: Finding Your Financial Confidence
by Eleanor Blayney
Written for clients, this book offers information and practical advice about the fundamentals of financial planning and how to increase financial confidence.

Online Resources

Daily Worth
http://www.dailyworth.com
This website provides women with a community to discuss money and offers practical and empowering ideas for approaching personal finances.

Directions for Women

http://www.DirectionsforWomen.com

This website was created by author Eleanor Blayney, a CFP dedicated to providing resources to improve and broaden financial advisors' outreach to women as well as to offer information so female consumers can make better financial decisions.

LearnVest

http://www.LearnVest.com

This website's mission is to empower women everywhere to take control of their personal finances so that they can afford their dreams. The website has various tools to help your female clients take action in this area.

The Women's Institute for Financial Education

http://www.wife.org

This is the oldest nonprofit organization dedicated to providing financial education to women in their quest for financial independence.

Financial Psychology

Books

Creating Wealth from the Inside Out Workbook and Audio Program

by Kathleen Burns Kingsbury

Written as a client resource, this workbook offers practical information and activities to help your clients change how they think and feel about money. Companion audio is narrated by the author and is a great introduction to the concepts in the workbook.

The Financial Wisdom of Ebenezer Scrooge

by Rick Kahler, Brad Klontz, and Ted Klontz

This book is easy to read and is written for the layperson. The authors show you how to recognize ways that unconscious money scripts may keep you trapped, how to deal with the relationship between your net worth and your self-worth, and how to leave a family legacy of financial wellness.

Your Money Style: The Nine Attitudes to Money and How They Affect Happiness, Love, Work, and Family

by Olivia Mellan

An innovative program developed by the author to help individuals and couples resolve their money conflicts, this book teaches you how to gain insight into your own money style by evaluating the impact of childhood experiences on your current money attitudes and behaviors.

Organizations

Financial Therapy Association
http://www.financialtherapyassociation.org
This is the first not-for-profit organization dedicated to discussing and researching the cognitive, emotional, behavioral, relational, and economic aspects of financial health. There is a forum for researchers, practitioners, the media, and policymakers to share research and practice methods and models of financial therapy. The organization hosts an annual conference and a publication titled *The Journal of Financial Therapy*.

Intergenerational and Family Wealth
Books

Wealth in Families
by Charles W. Collier
This is a very readable book written by a prominent wealth consultant for high-net-worth families, which provides advice on preserving good money skills across generations.

What If . . . Workbook
by Gwen Morgan
Created to serve as a comprehensive guide, this book assists individuals and families who are putting together their personal affairs and final wishes. It is a great tool for opening communication among family members.

Organizations

Family Firm Institute
http://www.ffi.org
The Family Firm Institute is the leading membership association worldwide for professionals who service the family enterprise field. The website has a list of local chapters, online resources, and articles, and a listing of professionals specializing in working with affluent families.

Marketing
Books

Why She Buys: The New Strategy for Reaching the World's Most Powerful Consumers
by Bridget Brennan
Brennan offers very practical advice, based on her expertise in marketing and advertising, for marketing and selling successfully to women.

Marketing to Women: How to Understand, Reach, and Increase Your Share of the World's Largest Market Segment
by Marti Barletta
This book shows why the women's market is the fastest track to strong business results in today's extraordinarily competitive environment and an increasingly important and powerful market segment which companies cannot afford to ignore.

What Women Want: The Global Market Turns Female Friendly
by Paco Underhill
Underhill offers a tour of the world's marketplace—with shrewd observations and practical applications to help everybody adapt to the new realities. He reports on the growing importance of women in everybody's marketplace—what makes a package, product, space, or service female friendly.

Mental Health
Books

To Buy or Not to Buy: Why We Overshop and How to Stop
by April Lane Benson
Drawing on recent research and on decades of working with overshoppers, Dr. April Benson brings together key insights with practical strategies in a powerful program to help clients stop overshopping.

Mind over Money: Overcoming the Money Disorders That Threaten Our Financial Health
by Brad Klontz and Ted Klontz
The authors look at why we overspend, undersave, and have anxiety around money. The reader learns to recognize negative and self-defeating patterns of thinking, and replace them with better, healthier ones that ultimately result in a better relationship with money and wealth.

Online Resources

Shopaholic No More
http://www.shopaholicnomore.com
Sponsored by April Lane Benson, PhD, author and expert on compulsive shopping, this website provides help and support for clients, training for professionals, and advocacy against overconsumption.

The Real Dope on Dealing with an Addict
http://www.dealingwithanaddict.com
This website is a companion to a book by the same name. It is a resource to help families with addiction find treatment and reclaim their lives. The site includes

coaching exercises, a community forum, and a blog with the latest information and resources for addicts and their loved ones.

Organizations

Multiservice Eating Disorders Association (MEDA)
http://www.medainc.org
This is a nonprofit organization dedicated to the prevention and treatment of eating disorders. The website has information for clients and families on treatment as well as educational and support groups.

National Eating Disorders Association (NEDA)
http://www.nationaleatingdisorders.org
This is a nonprofit organization dedicated to assisting individuals and families affected by eating disorders. The organization sponsors the National Eating Disorders Awareness Week each year and serves as a catalyst for prevention, cures, and access to quality care.

Parenting Affluent Children
Books

Raised for Richness: Teach Kids Money Skills for Life
by Karyn Hodgens
Hodgens shows parents how to get kids thinking beyond their piggy banks in order to have meaningful dialogue about issues related to money and illustrates how to empower kids as young as six to be in charge of their money.

Raising Financially Fit Kids
by Joline Godfrey
Providing a developmental map that covers 10 specific money skills, this book teaches children to master these skills by the time they reach age 18 and to become financially secure adults. The map gives parents a step-by-step approach to helping their kids become habitual savers, smart money managers, and responsible decision makers.

Raising an Emotionally Intelligent Child
by John Gottman
This book teaches parents how to help their children regulate their emotional world and develop emotional intelligence.

Organizations

Independent Means, Inc.
http://www.independentmeans.com
Independent Means is the national leader in providing financial education for children of high-net-worth families. The goal of all the programs is to teach the next generation how to be financially self-reliant while living a life of purpose and passion.

The Gallo Consulting Group
http://www.galloconsulting.com
This consulting group was founded by the husband and wife authors, Eileen and Jon Gallo, of the book *Silver Spoon Kids: How Successful Parents Raise Responsible Children*. They offer a blog, training, and workshops on how to create financially intelligent families.

Philanthropy
Organizations

Catalytic Women
http://www.catalyticwomen.com
This organization harnesses the economic power of thoughtful, intelligent women who give to our communities. It brings philanthropy professionals together who bring practical experience to helping individuals give wisely and with maximum impact. The programs included are: monthly speaking programs, an extensive on-line library on giving, online forums, and list serves and philanthropic consulting.

Women Philanthropy Institute (WPI)
http://www.philanthropy.iupui.edu/womensphilanthropyinstitute/
WPI is part of the Center of Philanthropy at Indiana University. The center provides a continuum of research-based educational services to inform donors, fundraisers, institutions, and other constituencies about women's philanthropy and to develop best practices.

The Center on Wealth and Philanthropy (CWP) at Boston College
http://www.bc.edu/research/cwp/
This multidisciplinary research center specializes in the study of spirituality, wealth, philanthropy, and other aspects of cultural life in an age of affluence. Founded in 1970, CWP is a recognized authority on the relationship between economic wherewithal and philanthropy, the motivations for charitable involvement, and the underlying meaning and practice of care.

Women in Transition
Books

ABCs of Divorce for Women
by Carol Ann Wilson and Ginita Wall
This book is cowritten by a CFP and a CPA. It teaches the reader what she needs to know to manage the changes in life before, during, and after divorce.

Moving Forward on Your Own: A Financial Guidebook for Widows
by Kathleen Rehl, PhD, CFP
This practical workbook helps widows be more confident, knowledgeable, and secure about their money matters during this transition.

On Grief and Grieving: Finding the Meaning of Grief Through the Five Stages of Loss
by Elisabeth Kübler-Ross and David Kessler
By the author of the classic book *On Death and Dying*, this follow-up book offers practical advice and inspiration for grieving clients.

Index

About the Author

Kathleen Burns Kingsbury is a wealth psychology expert and behavioral change specialist passionate about bridging the gap between advisors and clients. Her company, KBK Wealth Connection, teaches financial services professionals how to connect, communicate, and collaborate more effectively with their clients to increase client retention and improve profitability.

Kathleen is a faculty member of the Certified Private Wealth Advisor (CPWA) program, an educational course developed by the Investment Management Consultants Association (IMCA) and offered in conjunction with The University of Chicago Booth School of Business. She is also an adjunct lecturer at the McCallum Graduate School of Business at Bentley University, where she teaches the course "The Psychology of Financial Planning."

A frequent keynote speaker, Kathleen has presented at the Investment Management Consultants Association National Conference, Merrill Lynch Global Wealth and Investment Management Advanced Education Symposiums, Women Advisors Forums, the Massachusetts Bankers Association Wealth Management Conference, and various chapters of the Financial Planning Association. In addition, Kathleen has been engaged by financial firms, including Pioneer Investments, TD Ameritrade Institutional, and American Student Assistance, as a consultant and trainer.

Voted one of the top 10 executive coaches in 2009 by *Women's Business*, Kathleen is an internationally published author. Prior to writing *How to Give Financial Advice to Women*, she published a client workbook, *Creating Wealth from the Inside Out Workbook*. She is a columnist for the Women Advisors Forum and has contributed articles to print and online publications, including IMCA's *Investment and Wealth Monitor*, *MOTIVATED* magazine, and *The Glass Hammer*.

As an expert on financial psychology, Kathleen has been interviewed by the *Wall Street Journal*, *New York Times*, MSNBC's "Today Money," *Forbes's* "ForbesWoman," Thomson Reuters's "Reuters Wealth," and *Financial Planning* magazine. She is a frequent radio guest and has appeared on WBNW's "Money Matters Radio," WCBM's "Money, Riches & Wealth," and others.

Kathleen holds a masters in psychology and is a Certified Professional Co-Active Coach (CPCC). She is a member of the Financial Therapy Association, the International Coach Federation, and the National Speakers Association for which she has served on the Board of Directors of the New England chapter.

When she is not working, Kathleen is an avid alpine skier who lives for the next powder day. In the off-season, she enjoys road and mountain biking, kayaking, and sailing.

About KBK Wealth Connection

KBK Wealth Connection is a company dedicated to training, coaching, and consulting with financial services professionals. Founded in 2006, KBK helps financial advisors use wealth psychology to improve client communication, satisfaction, and retention and to increase the profitability of their practice. The company publishes resources for financial advisors and their clients, including articles, books, CDs, podcasts, and a blog. For more information, visit www. kbkwealthconnection.com.